Do it

alpha books

1. Line the grill box of your charcoal grill with aluminum foil for easy cleanup.

2. Don't start grilling over charcoal briquettes until the charcoal appears ash gray in daylight or glowing red at night.

3. To tame flare-ups, select leaner cuts of meat or trim as much fat from the meat as possible.

4. If meat chars, cut away the blackened portion to remove any possible carcinogens.

5. Precook poultry or ribs in the microwave or by boiling them the night before. Grill briefly for that "outdoors" flavor.

One luxurious bubble bath

Access to most comfortable chair and favorite TV show

One half-hour massage (will need to recruit spouse, child, friend)

Time to recline and listen to a favorite CD (or at least one song)

cut

6. Use non-stick griddles and grilling accessories for easy cleanup.

7. Marinate food inside Zip-lock plastic bags. Turn the bag occasionally to marinate all sides.

8. When you serve salad, arrange the outer leaves of kale or other greens on coated paper or plastic plates to create an attractive presentation.

9. Grill packet meals in easy-to-make foil containers.

10. Keep a box of baking soda near the grill to extinguish hard-to-control flames.

COUPON

COUPON

COUPON

COUPON

Master
the
Grill

Master
the
Grill

Pamela Rice Hahn
and Keith Giddeon

Macmillan • USA

To everyone who enjoys our recipes and humor and adopts *The Lazy Way.*

Macmillan General Reference books may be purchased for business or sales promotional use. For information please write: Special Markets Department, Macmillan Publishing USA, 1633 Broadway, New York, NY 10019.

International Standard Book Number: 0-02-863157-9
Library of Congress Catalog Card Number: 99-61544

01 00 99   8 7 6 5 4 3 2 1

Interpretation of the printing code: the rightmost number of the first series of numbers is the year of the book's printing; the rightmost number of the second series of numbers is the number of the book's printing. For example, a printing code of 99-1 shows that the first printing occurred in 1999.

Printed in the United States of America

Book Design: Madhouse Studios

Page Creation by Carrie Allen and Eric Brinkman

You Don't Have to Feel Guilty Anymore!

IT'S O.K. TO DO IT *THE LAZY WAY*!

It seems every time we turn around, we're given more responsibility, more information to absorb, more places we need to go, and more numbers, dates, and names to remember. Both our bodies and our minds are already on overload. And we know what happens next—cleaning the house, balancing the checkbook, and cooking dinner get put off until "tomorrow" and eventually fall by the wayside.

So let's be frank—we're all starting to feel a bit guilty about the dirty laundry, stacks of ATM slips, and Chinese takeout. Just thinking about tackling those terrible tasks makes you exhausted, right? If only there were an easy, effortless way to get this stuff done! (And done right!)

There is—*The Lazy Way*! By providing the pain-free way to do something—including tons of shortcuts and timesaving tips, as well as lists of all the stuff you'll ever need to get it done efficiently—*The Lazy Way* series cuts through all of the time-wasting thought processes and laborious exercises. You'll discover the secrets of those who have figured out *The Lazy Way*. You'll get things done in half the time it takes the average person—and then you will sit back and smugly consider those poor suckers who haven't discovered *The Lazy Way* yet. With *The Lazy Way,* you'll learn how to put in minimal effort and get maximum results so you can devote your attention and energy to the pleasures in life!

THE LAZY WAY PROMISE

Everyone on *The Lazy Way* staff promises that, if you adopt *The Lazy Way* philosophy, you'll never break a sweat, you'll barely lift a finger, you won't put strain on your brain, and you'll have plenty of time to put up your feet. We guarantee you will find that these activities are no longer hardships, since you're doing them *The Lazy Way*. We also firmly support taking breaks and encourage rewarding yourself (we even offer our suggestions in each book!). With *The Lazy Way*, the only thing you'll be overwhelmed by is all of your newfound free time!

THE LAZY WAY SPECIAL FEATURES

Every book in our series features the following sidebars in the margins, all designed to save you time and aggravation down the road.

- **"Quick 'n' Painless"**—shortcuts that get the job done fast.

- **"You'll Thank Yourself Later"**—advice that saves time down the road.

- **"A Complete Waste of Time"**—warnings that spare countless headaches and squandered hours.

- **"If You're So Inclined"**—optional tips for moments of inspired added effort.

- **"The Lazy Way"**—rewards to make the task more pleasurable.

If you've either decided to give up altogether or have taken a strong interest in the subject, you'll find information on hiring outside help with "How to Get Someone Else to Do It" as well as further reading recommendations in "If You Really Want More, Read These." In addition, there's an only-what-you-need-to-know glossary of terms and product names ("If You Don't Know What It Means, Look Here") as well as "It's Time for Your Reward"—fun and relaxing ways to treat yourself for a job well done.

With *The Lazy Way* series, you'll find that getting the job done has never been so painless!

Series Editor
Amy Gordon

Managing Editor
Robert Shuman

Editorial Director
Gary Krebs

Development Editor
Joan Paterson

Director of Creative Services
Michele Laseau

Production Editor
Jenaffer Brandt

Cover Designer
Michael Freeland

What's in This Book

Let the others bring home the bacon and fry it up in a pan, we'll avoid cleaning up the grease splatters—especially when we know that our meal prepared on the gas grill will require *no* cleanup. Whether you plan to use gas, charcoal, a smoker, or your electric countertop or stovetop grill, we'll show you how to maximize your results with minimum effort. Plus, as if that isn't enough, we believe you'll find that your food tastes better, too. Before you know it, you'll be grilling snacks, meals, and complex feasts in a snap.

Today Grilling Is So Easy, You Don't Have to Wait for a Flash of Inspiration

We imagine the first cookout occurred one day when, after a thunder-storm, cavemen (and women) from the Bar-B clan formed a queue around a wooly mammoth that had been zapped and charred by a bolt of lightning.

Once they tasted that fire-roasted flavor, mammoth tartare just didn't satisfy their palates anymore. Finding a way to duplicate that aroma and piquancy became as important as their hunting rituals. This was a can-do tribe!

So, because they were a forward-thinking group of nomads, they formed a committee. The committee then designated project teams, whose job it was to find ways to grill meat for the next feast. They round-ed up herds of animals and trapped them in the valley, while the more limber members on their team danced a rain dance around the perimeter. They herded those animals to different locations, just in case the rumors about frequent lightning strikes were true.

One day—tired and frustrated of being merely a link in a human fence, and also getting very hungry by this time—a junior member of the team took a break from his daydreams of becoming a freelance consultant and decided to make use of some loose rocks lying in the gully. First he stacked them in a spiral pattern that encompassed his tribe's understanding of their outreaching purpose of life on this planet, sacred geometry, and the Feng Shui dynamic he intended to write a book about once somebody developed a language. Eventually though, growing weary from his task, he stumbled on some loose stones and dropped a rock, which struck some flint, which kindled some twigs clinging to another rock, and the rest, as they say, is history. (Alas, his boss took credit for the discovery.)

However, this breakthrough not only led to expertly grilled meals (and arguments among alpha members of the clan as to whether or not the food was done yet), it also led to smoke signals, which evolved to other means of communications, which resulted in the Industrial Age, which made possible standardized grill construction, which eventually brought us to where we are today—hoping we now have your attention so you continue to not only read this book, but savor the recipes and have a good time in the process. Enjoy!

THANK YOU. . .

The authors would like to thank Kathryn Toler for introducing us to *The Lazy Way* series; Amy Gordon for her faith in this project; Joan Paterson for her wise edits and constructive assistance (and for laughing at our jokes); Amy Borelli for the copyedits; Jenaffer Brandt for getting every-thing ready so our book made it to production; our family and friends who not only sampled our grilled creations but cheered us on during this project and understood why, at times, we were a bit preoccupied; to our regular readers of The Blue Rose Bouquet (www.blueroses.com), who understand that we always eventually get the new issue online once we complete our "day job" writing work; and a special thanks to all of our online friends in #Authors on the Undernet (www.blueroses.com/authors/) who support and encourage us by celebrating each time we have good writing news.

Pam also thanks... Lara Sutton, daughter and joy of my life, for letting me fire up your grill for winter lunches. Granddaughter Taylor for your help making pizza crusts. Grandson Charlie for understanding that even though you are now getting teeth and want to put everything in your mouth, you need to be patient a bit longer. Nicole Teeters (my niece) and Michele Nagel (my "administrative assistant") for their help testing the recipes, especially when they did the dishes, too. Mom, Dad, and the sib-lings for being there. My computer guru buddy Don Lachey, friends at paintedrock.com, and others online—the elusive Bishop, David Hebert, Jodi Cornelius, Troy More, Steve Harris, and Ed Williams—for sharing the laughter. Janet Nelson for reminding me about some of my "creations" that we'd been too busy to grill in far too long. Prince Charming, wher-ever you are: Do I have a meal planned for you!

Keith also thanks... Mom and Dad for understanding that writing is an enjoyable and fulfilling career. Billy Padley, a friend of almost 20 years, who helped me with the testing of some recipes. Tammy Williams for the London Broil recipe in Chapter 8. Nicole Torgerson for reminding me that time off is a valuable commodity.

Pamela Rice Hahn

Keith Giddeon

The Perfect Pantry Planner

Are You Too Lazy to Read the Perfect Pantry Planner?

1 You use your pantry to store gift wrap and holiday decorations. ☐ yes ☐ no

2 You think Marinate is one of the Olson twins. ☐ yes ☐ no

3 You're only familiar with the herbs Simon and Garfunkel sing about. ☐ yes ☐ no

one

Simple Staples Sense

One of the secrets to grilling *The Lazy Way* is to keep your kitchen inventory under control. Knowing what foods you have on hand makes meal preparation so much easier. When you know what you have available, you can tuck this book into your attaché, carry it with you, and pull it out to search for your next meal's recipe while you wait in line or for the dentist to come into the room. (If you're waiting for the dentist to come in to perform a root canal, we recommend that you prepare a soft food, such as haggis or stuffed mushrooms, as your main course.)

But that's getting ahead of ourselves. Before that suggestion becomes practical, you must first determine what you already have on hand in your kitchen and what items you need to buy. Stop complaining! This will only take a few minutes, and once you've completed this task, you'll save yourself time later—maybe even enough to indulge in a bubble bath or read something other than a cookbook. (Enough time for a nightly massage depends on the cooperation of others within your household or group of friends; that option we leave entirely to your discretion.)

Got that notebook and pen at the ready? Good, because it's inventory time! Ready. Set. Go!

IN THE CUPBOARD AND PANTRY

Putting staples on your shelves doesn't mean tacking the shelf paper into place.

On one hand, some foods you should buy fresh. Foodstuffs, on the other hand, are things that, if you want to be practical, you must keep in stock. As contradictory as it may sound, keeping both of those hands involved now will save you from juggling some steps later.

Bare Necessities

Storage won't be a problem for most of the items on this list because many of them come in their own sturdy containers, designed for just that purpose. Naturally, you can keep baking soda longer than bakery items—otherwise, you'll end up with marbled "wry" bread. Expiration dates are on those packages for a reason. Use those dates and your cooking style and quantity to gauge how much to buy to maintain your "live" stock.

- Arrowroot
- Baking powder
- Baking soda (Keep extra on hand to make a paste to clean the grill. See Chapter 5.)
- Bread, such as crusty loaves of French bread and bakery sandwich buns
- Broth mix or cubes (See Appendix A for information on our preferred method to make instant broth; we

keep our broth bases in the refrigerator, but if you insist on using cubes, it's okay to keep them in the pantry.)

- Canned tomatoes (whole or chopped)
- Cornstarch
- Flour (The measurements in our recipes, such as those for pizza crusts, call for white or unbleached flour, but there's no reason why you can't substitute stone-ground whole wheat for a portion of that flour, if you prefer.)
- Honey
- Maple syrup
- Olive oil (extra-virgin olive oil for salads and regular for use in marinades)
- Pasta
- Peanut butter
- Rice (white, brown, or wild)
- Salt (You'll notice as you read this book that we use very little salt. Even when a recipe requires it, we use the minimum amount possible. Keep the shaker at the table so those whose tastes require more can add it.)
- Soy sauce (We stock both Kikkoman and La Choy; each brand has its own distinct flavor, which is why we often blend them to create a subtle, yet distinct, difference in our recipes.)
- Sugar (white—we prefer cane—and brown)

IF YOU'RE SO INCLINED

The Lazy Way doesn't mean you sacrifice flavor. That's why we recommend you purchase natural peanut butter and real maple syrup. You, your family, and your guests will appreciate the purer and better taste.

You'll find recipes throughout this book calling for different kinds of vinegars. Stocking up now saves you time later. Feel free to experiment, too, such as adding a splash of balsamic vinegar and a little sugar to perk up deli potato salad.

- Tahini (sesame seed paste—available in toasted and regular)

- Toasted sesame oil (for adding flavor to Asian dishes)

- Vegetable oil (corn, peanut, canola, sesame, or other poly- or mono-unsaturated oil; we prefer olive oil for almost everything, but occasionally a milder oil is called for. Peanut oil can better withstand higher temperatures, for example, for those times you want to use an oil to fry something atop the grill in a grill-safe or cast-iron skillet.)

- Vinegar (You can never have too many varieties of vinegar: red wine, white wine, cider, rice wine, flavored and infused, and balsamic.)

- Worcestershire sauce (For the same reasons we keep different soy sauce brands on hand, we also stock both French's and Lea & Perrins.)

Useful Pantry Extras

Even if your home doesn't have a designated pantry area, you can still reserve a corner of your cupboard for special ingredients. Keeping some out-of-the-ordinary items at the ready will help you create extraordinary meals.

- Canned peppers, such as chipotle or roasted red pepper (See Appendix A for the concentrates we use instead.)

- Black olives

- Canned broth (See Appendix A for our preferred alternative to canned broth; we use bases instead.)
- Chocolate chips (semi-sweet)
- Cocoa
- Hoisin sauce
- Instant mashed potatoes
- Kosher salt
- Marshmallows
- Molasses
- Oatmeal
- Oyster sauce
- Popcorn
- Powdered or canned evaporated milk
- Raisins
- Shelled nuts (pecans, walnuts, peanuts, almonds, sesame seeds)
- Tomato paste and puree
- Vanilla (only real vanilla, please, not imitation)
- Wines and liqueurs for cooking (red, white, sherry, Kahlua)

Spices and Herbs

Unless we state otherwise, the recipes throughout this book call for dried herbs and spices.

- Allspice
- Basil
- Bay leaves

A COMPLETE WASTE OF TIME

The 3 Worst Things You Can Do with Canned Chicken Broth:

1. Store the unused portion too long.

2. Cut your finger on the can.

3. Forget that you can use the leftover amount in place of some of the water when you prepare rice.

QUICK n PAINLESS

If a recipe calls for a fruit liqueur you don't have on hand, you don't have to rush out and buy some. Simply substitute some frozen fruit juice concentrate instead.

- Cayenne pepper
- Chili powder
- Cilantro (sometimes called Chinese parsley)
- Cinnamon
- Cloves
- Cumin
- Dill
- Fennel seed
- Garlic powder
- Grated lemon peel
- Grated orange peel
- Marjoram
- Minced, dried onion
- Mint
- Mustard, dry
- Nutmeg
- Old Bay Seasoning blend (see recipe)
- Onion powder
- Oregano
- Paprika
- Parsley
- Peppercorns, black
- Red pepper flakes
- Rosemary
- Sage
- Thyme

Old Bay Seasoning

1 tablespoon celery seed

1 tablespoon whole black peppercorns

6 bay leaves

$^1/_2$ teaspoon whole cardamom

$^1/_2$ teaspoon mustard seed

4 whole cloves

1 teaspoon sweet Hungarian paprika

$^1/_4$ teaspoon mace

1 In a spice grinder or small food processor, combine all of the ingredients.

2 Grind well and store in a small glass jar.

IN THE REFRIGERATOR

If you have kids, you've probably often wondered why you bothered installing an air conditioner, considering how much time they spend standing in front of the refrigerator, supposedly staring at the contents. (We suspect it was once a tip in a fashion magazine, its origination lost in time, but now it's the method teenage girls use to set their makeup so it doesn't run on hot summer days.)

You spend your share of time staring into an open refrigerator, too. But you're looking for answers to that age-old question: Whatever do I fix to eat tonight? Here are some of the things you should find whenever you open the door.

IF YOU'RE SO INCLINED

It isn't always possible or convenient, but when you can, you'll find that using freshly ground spices instead of the prepackaged variety gives a taste difference comparable to fresh instead of instant coffee. Try our recipe for Old Bay Seasoning and see for yourself!

Bare Necessities

Just because you store something in the refrigerator doesn't mean you can forget to watch the expiration date. It's funny when someone on a television sitcom grabs "soured" milk off the shelf; it's not quite as humorous when it happens to you.

- Milk
- Eggs
- Butter (We seldom use margarine, but it's your call when it comes to that.)
- Cheese (Always have cheddar and Parmesan on hand!)
- Jelly (grape, red currant, strawberry, apple butter)
- Catsup
- Mayonnaise
- Mustard (Dijon and regular)
- Salad dressing

Useful Extras

We named one of our chapters "Variety is the Nice of Life" for a reason. Subtle changes can convert your dish from a dull *same ol'-same ol'* one to something truly special. The ingredients we mention here will help nudge you out of that stuck-in-a-rut cooking mode.

- Buttermilk
- Cottage cheese
- Orange or other fruit juice

IF YOU'RE SO INCLINED

Don't be afraid to try making your own mayonnaise. It's another way to add that special flavor advantage to a dish. However, to be safe and avoid any possible salmonella contamination, we recommend you use pasteurized egg products instead of raw eggs.

- Mushrooms
- Salsa
- Soda
- Sparkling water

Treat Yourself

Every family has a picky eater. It must be one of the rules. Using the items we recommend here will garner a five-star rating from even the most finicky food critic.

- Fresh pasta
- Cream (Because of its high fat content, cream will keep for weeks. It only takes a small amount to make a delicious difference in your soups and sauces.)
- Olives
- Pickles (dill, sweet, candied sweet, bread and butter)
- Sauces and condiments (barbecue, chili, chutney, pesto)

IN THE FREEZER

Whenever possible, use fresh foods to prepare your meal. But because it's impossible to plan for every possibility (unexpected guests or the kids bringing home a few friends), keeping extra vegetables, fruit juice concentrates, and meats in the freezer will save you unwanted trips to the store. The nice thing about a freezer is that it allows you to buy those products when they're on sale and keep them stored until you need them.

YOU'LL THANK YOURSELF LATER

What do you do if a recipe calls for buttermilk and you don't have any on hand? You can buy it in dry powder form. Or, some find it easier to substitute plain yogurt instead.

Freeze steaks and pork chops in packages containing the number you need to feed your family per meal.

- Bread dough (to use for pizza crust when you don't have time to make your own)
- Chicken (flash-frozen boneless, skinless breasts and thighs)
- Fish fillets
- Ground pork and sausage
- Hamburger
- Hot dogs
- Ice
- Shrimp
- Steak and pork chops
- Tortillas (flour and corn)
- Vegetables

FRESH VEGETABLES

There are vegetables you can always keep on hand. Others, such as seasonal fresh sweet corn or squash, you'll pick up on the day you need them. The nice thing about most vegetables is, unless we note otherwise, you don't have to store them in the refrigerator.

Bare Necessities

Preparing your meals *The Lazy Way* doesn't mean you do so at the expense of "the healthy way." Keep crisp, fresh veggies on hand for when you get the munchies or to use in your salads and grilled side dishes. Here are some "healthy way" foods we recommend you keep in stock.

- Carrots (Store in the refrigerator.)
- Celery (Store in the refrigerator, and keep in mind that even when this vegetable goes limp, you can still use it in most cooking.)
- Cucumbers (Store in the refrigerator.)
- Garlic (Even if you use the prepared sautéed and roasted garlic concentrates we mention in Appendix A, you'll still want fresh garlic to rub in salad bowls.)
- Green onions (scallions)
- Lettuce (You must keep this in the refrigerator crisper. And don't get stuck in an iceburg rut! Use a variety, such as romaine, Bibb, or fresh spinach.)
- Onions (yellow and white)
- Potatoes (baking, red, and sweet)

Useful Extras

So you can add flavor that you'll savor, include these items on your shopping list, too.

- Cabbage (best stored in the refrigerator, especially after it's been cut)
- Ginger (fresh root or candied)
- Peppers (green or red; refrigerate)
- Shallots

Treat Yourself

Go ahead and buy whatever vegetables are in season. We give plenty of suggestions on how to grill sweet corn, squash, tomatoes, and other special, seasonal vegetables.

QUICK ☞ PAINLESS

Blanche a package of frozen mixed vegetables and toss them together with some pasta and salad dressing for a quick salad.

IN THE FRUIT BOWL

Unless we tell you otherwise, you can keep most fruit nestled in a bowl, where it not only looks attractive but will also be in view so you and your family will grab it first when looking for a snack, instead of hunting through the pantry for that package of cookies or chips.

Bare Necessities

Many people are surprised to learn that fruit isn't just for snacks and desserts. It can be used in grilled dishes, to add pizzazz to salsa, and in other ways, as you'll discover throughout this book. Here are some we suggest you keep on hand.

- Apples
- Bananas
- Grapefruit
- Lemons (These keep longer in the refrigerator.)
- Oranges

Useful Extras

Don't leave out what we like to think of as special occasion fruit. You can either grill the ones we suggest below or serve them fresh for dessert. Everybody likes a treat now and then.

- Grapes
- Kiwi fruit
- Limes (These keep longer in the refrigerator.)

- Pears
- Plums (These keep longer in the refrigerator.)

Treat Yourself

For us, "in season" is dictated by our cravings. Whether you buy these fruits fresh or use them freshly thawed, they'll add a wonderful touch to any meal.

- Blackberries
- Blueberries
- Strawberries
- Raspberries

When you keep your kitchen well stocked, half of the "what'll I cook tonight?" dilemma is already solved. You'll find that a quick peek at what's on hand will trigger menu ideas. When that happens, cooking is no longer a chore, but a pleasure. And everybody likes to have fun. So, have a ball! You deserve it.

YOU'LL THANK YOURSELF LATER

The checkout lane scanner updates the store's inventory. Post your grocery list in a convenient place, train each family member to make a note when she or he uses the last of an item, and you'll keep your kitchen inventory under control as well.

Getting Time on Your Side

	The Old Way	The Lazy Way
Planning a meal	30 minutes	5 minutes
Preparing a grocery list	30 minutes	1 minute (the time it takes to grab it off the fridge and take it with you)
Trips to the store	Once per meal	Once or twice a week
Gathering ingredients	60 minutes	5 minutes
Readying food for the grill	60 minutes	30 minutes or less
Time left over to spend on a relaxing, leisurely meal	5 minutes	60 minutes (cocktail before, savoring the meal, and coffee or brandy afterwards)

Effortless Equipment Education

With almost any activity or hobby, there are certain items that we "must" have in order to participate. Of course, there is always the minimum required equipment; it's the extras which can usually (if we don't control ourselves) drop us into debt, the likes of which haven't been seen since the Great Depression. We simply have to control ourselves. Some things are necessary while others aren't.

This chapter will give you ideas on which equipment you need to accomplish the grilling techniques explained later in this book. We will also give you a few ideas on extra equipment which can save you time and worry, and help avoid those occasional instances when you want to drop to the floor kicking and screaming when something doesn't turn out "just" right.

Okay, ready? Sit back, lovingly pat your wallet or purse—this won't hurt, we promise (maybe).

A grill is an important tool which you'll own for a long time. Take your time, comparison shop and look at all the features, and get the one right for you. Treat yourself by getting the best one you can afford on your budget.

FOR WHOM THE GRILL COOKS

We have an easy question for you. What is the most essential thing you need in order to GRILL food? Right! Hey, you're good.

If a grill were just a grill, things would be simple. As it turns out, though, grills come in different varieties and sizes. All you have to do is decide which is best for your needs. Don't worry, it's not as difficult as it might seem at first. We won't be going into great detail about the grills themselves. Everyone pretty much has their own opinion about which type is better.

A good place to see many grills side-by-side for your selection is at a local hardware "superstore" or at a national department store in your area. The salespeople there can answer any specific questions you might have about a certain model or grills in general.

There are basically four types of grills: gas, charcoal, electric (indoor and outdoor), and built-in pits. In this chapter, we are going to limit ourselves to gas and charcoal grills. Why, you ask? Well, electric indoor grills are usually very small, creating a tedious process if you have a lot of food to cook. True, the larger outdoor electric grills are very similar in use to their gas counterparts. But we feel the best "grilling experience" can be had with a charcoal or gas grill.

Next, there's nothing "lazy" about lugging bricks and mortar around in order to build a pit when you can go out and buy a grill in less than an hour (depending where you live), so we'll avoid pit grills.

TO GAS OR NOT TO GAS? IS THAT A QUESTION?

There are advantages and disadvantages to using a gas grill.

Advantages: Using a gas grill gives you better control over temperature during the preparation of foods. How so? With KNOBS! Some only have one or two knobs, while others look as if they could easily control a starship from your favorite science-fiction show. In addition, gas grills have igniter switches which, well…ignite the gas for you. This is a welcome alternative to hunting down matches or a lighter and then lowering your hand to "ground zero" when lighting the grill. How about that? No more spastic, spine-tingling reactions when the flame ignites!

With a gas grill, you don't have to worry about remembering to buy charcoal, and then arranging it. Plus, compared to the cost of charcoal, gas is the most economical choice. You can replace your canister for about $10 and get many uses from it. Charcoal briquettes cost $2 to $5 per bag, depending on quality and size. This cost rises if you get unique briquettes, like the kind with exotic woods included, from a specialty store.

Disadvantages: There are two disadvantages worth noting to using a gas cooker. With gas (unless you have purchased materials to counter this problem), you don't get the flavor of charcoal-cooked foods. We will discuss how to overcome this later in the chapter. Secondly, the price of gas grills is well above that of their charcoal

QUICK ⬤ PAINLESS

Always be sure to have a spare gas tank (filled) or bag of charcoal on hand. Nothing can be more frustrating than running out of fuel in the middle of grilling.

counterparts. But, as we've heard most of our lives, "you get what you pay for." This may or may not be true in some cases, but we believe it is when it comes to grills.

Recommendation: If you can afford the higher price and adding wood chips (discussed later) for flavor is no prob- lem for you, gas grills are the way to go, in our humble opinion. They cook food more evenly and accurately, and with proper maintenance will last much longer than their charcoal cousins.

IT'S MY CHARCOAL AND I'LL BUY IF I WANT TO

We hope you're like us and love to grill food with an obsession. However, if you're only a grill chef for special events, a charcoal grill will be the best choice for you. The low price of most varieties of these cookers, coupled with the small amount of maintenance they require, is usually best in this case.

THE RIGHT TOOLS FOR ANY GRILL

Simply owning a grill is not enough. Sure, they look nice just sitting there, waiting to be used. But, like a baseball player needs more than a field to play upon, so it goes with the serious grill chef. Some things are necessary while others are just extras—"toys," if you will. In this section, we'll show you a different variety of tools to make your grilling experience more enjoyable. We'll even suggest which tools to always have handy, and mention those you can either get or live without (if you absolutely must do so).

Utensils You Will Need

Unless you're impervious to the pain of heat and flames (unlike us), you're going to need a few items to assist in the turning and basting of food as it sits on the cooking grid.

- Tongs are very handy for turning items that are bulky and not necessarily flat, such as poultry and large vegetables like potatoes and eggplant. These are a must-have item.

- A spatula with a long handle is always necessary when cooking hamburgers or any other flat-sided food item. The longer the handle, the better. Remember, we're cooking the food, not our hands and lower arms.

- A long-handled, two-pronged fork is a great item to have around during steak season (which is year-round, of course!). These also come in handy while turning thick pork chops.

- An absolute necessity is a good quality basting brush. Actually, owning more than one might prove to be of tremendous help if you'll be cooking more than one type of meat at once. This also saves you from washing a brush before using it again near the completion of the cooking time; you need a clean brush then to avoid cross-contamination.

- A sauce mop is exactly what the name implies. It looks like a regular household mop, except it's much smaller. It holds much more sauce than a basting brush. This can be very useful when cooking large

YOU'LL THANK YOURSELF LATER

Tongs also come in the long-handled variety. This keeps you back as far away as possible from the grill and lessens the chances you'll get singed should there be a flare-up.

amounts of ribs or whole birds. A mop isn't absolutely necessary, since you can use a brush, but it can save you some time when there's a lot of basting involved.

- Special two-pronged skewers are invaluable when making kabobs. Food is placed on one prong while the second holds it in place with pressure. Food will no longer rotate on the skewer while you're turning it!

- A meat thermometer is an absolute necessity! Not only will using one allow you to tell when food is done, but it's important to be sure the meat has reached the proper internal temperature to kill any harmful bacteria which could cause sickness.

Accessorize Yourself

Using our example from above, what if a baseball catcher entered a game without his protective cup? There's a potential "Ouch!" in the making, huh? Well, just like those guys, we need to take some precautions as well. Below is some equipment you should consider acquiring to guarantee your days of grilling are safe ones.

- Grilling mitts are a great way to assure yourself and others that you're cooking what needs to be cooked and nothing else! Grills have a funny way of getting hot in the strangest places. Who would've thought?

- Okay, picture it. You've become more daring in front of your grill; there's sauce and meat flying in all directions as you baste and turn like a true pro! Why

not prevent staining your clothes, and possibly getting a few short stinging burns, by wearing a good apron? Aprons come in several designs and are made of different materials. You decide, cloth or plastic, full or half-length. Remember, though, keep it tied tightly. You don't want it catching on fire!

GRILL ACCESSORIES

If you look around, you'll find a multitude of grill accessories at specialty and department stores. We are going to describe some in the following sections. These products are designed to make your grilling experience easier by solving specific problems inherent to cooking on a grid with gas or charcoal.

Toppers and Griddles

Grill toppers are special add-on grids or surfaces that usually have a specific purpose. They have small gaps (none for griddles) in the cooking area and are placed on a grill's cooking surface. They come in various sizes and range in price from $6 to $15. With these you can cook smaller, delicate foods like fish, shrimp, vegetables and bite-sized pieces of pork, poultry or beef. There are also special toppers for unique foods.

- For those of you who like Oriental cuisine, also available is a wok topper that can be used to prepare— you guessed it—your favorite stir-fry recipes.

- How would you like to cook a complete breakfast on your grill? It's not impossible. You see, to keep the eggs from dripping through the grid, there's a

IF YOU'RE SO
INCLINED

Although some companies make mitts designed especially for grilling, regular oven mitts work just as well.

simple solution. Pick up a porcelain griddle, which rests on top of the cooking grid, and some egg rings. You'll be creating a smoky-flavored breakfast in no time at all.

■ You'll get hooked on the grilled pizza techniques later in this book. Guess what? There's a special pizza topper available just for that!

Internal Accessories

There are many add-ons for grills. Below we give a few examples to get you started. As you get more involved in grilling, you'll discover others.

■ Want to add that "real" grilled taste to gas-cooked foods? Try a smoker box filled with mesquite, hickory, or your favorite soaked wood chips to achieve that perfect dining experience. Simply place the smoker box over the lava rocks (diffusing material) or briquettes in your grill.

■ For a larger gas grill, an electric rotisserie kit can be a great addition to save you some time while cooking whole birds, ribs, or whatever will fit on it. The food is automatically turned for you, which leaves you free to sit back and watch your favorite television show. Once in a while (during a commercial, of course) baste the meat if necessary.

■ A grill basket allows you to place several ears of corn, hamburgers, fish fillets, or any type of food so you can turn all of the items over at once. This will assure even cooking on all items.

- To get even more food on your grill, try a vertical roasting rack. These are great when grilling whole meals at once. One of these could double or triple the allowable cooking space contained on your grill.

External Accessories

If you wish, there are things you can add to the outside of your grill to save time or alleviate any needless worry, such as straining to see your food at night or worrying about clouds approaching, among other things. We'll give you some ideas for things you might consider getting to avoid these problems.

- While cooking at night, is it difficult to see when checking the doneness of your food? Try a grill light! It attaches to your grill and assures you'll be able to tell when to make the most important of grilling decisions: placing the food on the serving plate.

- It's happened to everyone. You've gone beyond a point of no return when cooking on the grill and rain clouds approach. Whatever should one do? Get a grill umbrella and end those worries. They are attached directly to the grill to ensure your food is soggy ONLY from the sauce or marinade you've used on it.

- One of the best ways to increase the chances that your grill has a long life ahead of it is to use a grill cover. This will protect it from the elements and reduce the chances of exterior corrosion. Remember to always let the grill cool down before replacing

Keep a damp cloth or paper towels handy for quick cleanup. That way, instead of running back and forth, you can treat yourself to a cold drink while you sit back and talk to friends and family.

The Lazy Way

the cover to minimize the chances of fire or damage to the cover.

- A handy way to discover the inside temperature of a grill is to obtain a grill thermometer. The dial remains outside the casing of the grill while the element is placed inside. This is one of the best ways to determine cooking time.

- There are a number of shelves and holders which allow you to safely place cooking supplies and tools within easy reach while keeping them out of your way. There are too many to mention here, so find the one(s) that suit you the best. There's nothing like a clutter-free cooking area.

THINGS YOU'LL NEED IN YOUR KITCHEN

There are some items we mention frequently that you'll need to have on hand to create the recipes in this book. We'll name a few, even though you'll probably already have them.

- A selection of glass bowls or casserole dishes of different sizes. These will be used mainly for marinades.

- Measuring cups and spoons to precisely measure the ingredients listed in the recipes.

- Glass jars with lids to store those leftover marinades and sauces in the refrigerator.

- Large Zip-lock plastic bags for marinating cuts of meat you'll need to turn often. These are handy because they allow you to "squeeze" the marinade around the food.

When you use a lot of glassware and utensils, the cleanup can seem to be an overwhelming task. Not if you prepare ahead of time and keep *The Lazy Way* spirit. Chapter 5 will give you many tips on how simple "Minimizing the Mess" can be for you.

EASY TIPS ON EQUIPMENT SAFETY

Grilling is, and always should be, fun. However, there are some safety concerns you need to remember. If you keep the following things in mind, you can assure that your cookout will not only be enjoyable, but safe, too. Try to keep all long-remembered family memories of your cookouts happy ones.

- Don't place your grill underneath a tree in your yard. During the dry season this could be a fire in the making.

- Remember, you're using open flames to cook your food. Anytime there are open flames, there's always a possibility of something going wrong. ALWAYS have a fire extinguisher handy when cooking on a grill. Keep your extinguisher a few feet away from the grill so you can get to it while avoiding any flames. And, as a backup, consider also getting the fifty-cent one we describe in Chapter 4.

- Always place your grill on a level surface. You don't want it tipping over or rolling away while you're cooking.

IF YOU'RE SO
INCLINED

Dedicate a shelf near the back door or have a special box to store your grilling supplies. You'll save time trying to hunt these items down, giving you more time to relax.

- Allow for some wind protection around your grill. High flames being blown by wind can either melt or set objects on fire around the grill.

- Keep extra bottles of fuel stored in a safe place. Always make sure the gas nozzle (the valve handle on top of the bottle) is turned off. Also, when your grill is not in use, make sure its bottle's nozzle is turned off.

- Get an old coffee can or something similar and place some sand in it, then get in the habit of throwing extinguished matches into it.

- Teach young children that a grill is not a toy and gets hot during use. We wouldn't want any burned fingers or worse.

- Unless you're using a grill specifically designed for the purpose, never grill indoors for any reason.

- Be sure to read all instructions and manuals that come with your grill and its accessories. There may be some model-specific safety concerns.

Following these tips and others in your manufacturer's documentation should assure you have happy grilling days ahead. Be sure to remember them, and that your friends and family know them, too.

Getting Time on Your Side

	The Old Way	The Lazy Way
Cleaning up small spills	15 minutes (for the trips back and forth to the kitchen to retrieve a damp cloth)	3 minutes (using the paper towels you keep handy)
Basting ribs with barbecue sauce	10 minutes	3 minutes (using a sauce mop)
Dealing with fire	30 minutes (includes the 911 call to the fire department and their arrival time)	30 seconds (the time it takes to grab the fire extinguisher, if necessary)
Grilling pancakes	60 minutes (on the grill rack to make enough long, skinny ones to feed your family)	5 minutes (making the same amount on your grill topper)
Chasing after your grill as it rolls down a hill	5 minutes	0 minutes (now that it's securely positioned on a level surface)
Minutes of fun in every grilling hour	5 minutes	60 minutes (okay—occasionally only 59)

Part 2

The Grilling Gourmet's Express: Tips

Are You Too Lazy to Read the Grilling Gourmet's Express?

1 Since that embarrassing incident the last time you used a grill, you promised the local fire department you'd study before your next cook-out. ☐ yes ☐ no

2 You think tongs include lyrics. ☐ yes ☐ no

3 You're convinced that Santa is the only one who actually makes a list and checks it twice. ☐ yes ☐ no

Getting a Grip on Grilling

Many people swear by charcoal, insisting that the flavor it gives meat and poultry is far superior to that achieved when food is grilled over a gas flame. The thinking is that charcoal imparts a smoky flavor that you just can't get from a gas-generated flame.

Surprisingly (to many), taste tests prove that isn't always the case. Many can't discern between flavors when it comes to hamburgers, skinless and boneless poultry cuts, and other fast-grilling foods. Meats that take longer to grill are another story. It makes sense that the longer the food is on the grill, the longer it has to absorb the fiery flavor. However, a charcoal fire may take longer to coax than a gas one; you can decide for yourself whether or not it's time well spent.

To help you with that decision and others, in this chapter we'll provide advice on selecting charcoal and your grilling method (direct, indirect, or packet meals), and offer other steps to help you plan ahead.

We're here to light a fire under you, so to speak, and get you started. Let's begin!

DON'T YOU HAVE ANYTHING IN A NICE PASTEL? CHOOSING THE CHARCOAL

Traditional charcoal briquettes are the most popular choice for grilling because their uniform shape and size help to distribute heat evenly during cooking. Others prefer the simplicity of flavored charcoal. Usually similar in size to standard briquettes, flavored briquettes contain ground mesquite or hickory wood added to the traditional material that imparts an authentic wood-smoke flavor to meat, poultry and fish. Many combine the flavored ones with their regular briquettes for a more subtle smoky flavor.

Lump charcoal, or lump char as it is sometimes known, is actually charred wood which, due to its resulting nonuniform shape, tends to burn less evenly. It also burns hotter than regular briquettes, cools faster, and occasionally sparks. Because this charcoal is more difficult to control, it's best to only use it for fast-grilling items, such as burgers. Keep in mind that because of the short time that food spends on the grill, most won't be able to distinguish any difference in its flavor over that prepared above a gas flame. Therefore, lump char is really only practical when using a hibachi, and a fast flame and short-lived coals are your goals.

Once you've determined the *type* of charcoal you wish to use, you need to decide *how much* charcoal you actually need. There are several ways you can build your fire.

For direct grilling (described below), you'll eventually want to spread the coals in a single layer barely touching each other, extending 2 inches beyond where the food will cook. When it comes to indirect grilling (also described below), your coals will either surround a drip pan or be grouped on one side of the grill.

As you've probably surmised by this point, determining in advance the amount of charcoal you'll need is not an exact science. You must factor in the size of your grill, your cooking method, and your grilling time and temperature. Don't let this overwhelm you. You'll eventually learn the science of your grill and someday get beyond the trial and error required in the early stages. To further help you with this learning process, be sure to see the information on lighting the fire, determining when the coals are ready, controlling the coals, using wood chips to add smoke flavor, and the other tips discussed in Chapter 4.

GRILLING METHODS FOR YOUR OUTDOOR COOKING MADNESS

When we travel, the direct route is usually the shortest distance between two points; the indirect one sometimes includes some trips around the barn. We plan that itinerary according to the mode of transportation, time elements, and other factors.

So it is when we grill. As you'll discover in this section, sometimes the best path to a succulently grilled

YOU'LL THANK YOURSELF LATER

To simplify the cleanup process, first line the firebox with aluminum foil. Then, once the coals have cooled, you can fold the foil up and over the ashes for easy disposal. Never douse the coals with water, or the extreme heat difference will warp the grill.

entrée is via a direct one; other times we can afford to be more subtle and use an indirect method.

Direct Grilling

The *direct method* is just what it sounds like—grilling your food directly over the flame or coals. Because it employs a hotter grilling temperature, you'll use this method for cuts of meat and other foodstuffs that will cook quickly.

Indirect Grilling

The *indirect method* is most often used in a covered grill, or with the food grilled under an aluminum foil "tent." And as the name implies, the food does not sit directly over the flame.

If you're using a charcoal grill, employ the appropriate utensil (such as the long-handled tongs mentioned in Chapter 2) to arrange medium coals around a drip pan into which you've poured water to a depth of 1 inch. Insert a meat thermometer (again see Chapter 2) into the meat and place it fat side up over the drip pan. Lower the grill hood and cook for the suggested time or until the meat thermometer registers the desired temperature.

On a gas grill, you'll keep the flame on one half of your grill and place your food on the other half. Depending on whether or not it's practical to rearrange the "lava rocks" on your gas grill or if it can accommodate a drip pan under the grill rack, you'll either follow the instructions similar to those given for the charcoal

QUICK ⬤ PAINLESS

When you grill meat or poultry using the direct method, flip it over after it's lost its pink color on top—usually about three-fourths of the way through the recommended grilling time. Then finish it off for a minute or two on the other side.

grill or simply place a pan of water on the rack over the flame. The latter is the method you'd use on an electric grill, too.

Special Effects

Unless you're using a smoker box as described in Chapter 2, the *smoking method* involves soaking wood chips for an hour and placing them directly on the hot coals. Most often, for this use of wood chips to be practical, you'll use the indirect grilling method. Plan on adding additional wood chips every 15 minutes throughout the grilling time. See Chapter 4 for some tips on prolonging the life of your wood chips.

Spit roasting is achieved with the use of a rotisserie and is probably the oldest open-flame roasting method. The cavemen probably used it to prepare a succulent leg of mammoth. Read your grill instructions. Some grills allow for a rotisserie attachments; it isn't necessary for other grills (such as the Weber Genesis or Platinum series grills) because they're already designed to allow for even roasting.

Grilling Terminology

Open grill is usually associated with backyard brick barbecues, hibachis, and inexpensive charcoal grills. However, for quick-grilling foods such as hamburgers, hot dogs, and thinner cuts of steak, you can achieve this grilling method by leaving the lid open. Simple enough.

Covered grill, as the name implies, is the method used for foods that take a longer grilling time, regardless

YOU'LL THANK YOURSELF LATER

Create a drip pan from an 18-inch wide piece of heavy duty aluminum foil. Tear off a length of foil about 6 inches long plus twice the length of the food the drip pan will sit under. Fold in half lengthwise. Fold all 4 sides in about 2 inches from the edge, flatten the folds, pull up the edges, and crimp the corners together to form the box. The pan will resemble a fitted box lid when you're done.

of whether you're using the direct or indirect grilling method.

GRILLING CHARTS: HELPING YOU MAP YOUR METHODS

Once you've determined the best method to use for grilling your entrée, you can estimate the grilling time that's required by consulting the appropriate chart below. (See Chapter 13 for the recommended grilling times for vegetables.)

Direct Grilling: Meat

Cut	Thickness (inches)	Grill Temperature	Doneness	Time (minutes)
Beef				
Flank steak	$3/4$	Medium	Medium	12 to 14
Steak	1	Medium	Rare	14 to 16
Chuck	1	Medium	Medium	18 to 20
Blade	1	Medium	Well-done	22 to 24
Top Round	$1^1/2$	Medium	Rare	19 to 26
	$1^1/2$	Medium	Medium	27 to 32
	$1^1/2$	Medium	Well-done	33 to 38
Strip Steak	1	Medium-hot	Rare	8 to 12
Top Loin	1	Medium-hot	Medium	12 to 15
Tenderloin	1	Medium-hot	Well-done	16 to 20
T-Bone	$1^1/2$	Medium-hot	Rare	14 to 18
Sirloin, Rib, Rib Eye	$1^1/2$	Medium-hot	Well-done	24 to 28
Porterhouse	$1^1/2$	Medium-hot	Medium	18 to 22

Indirect grilling, sometimes called the indirect method, is used for larger cuts of meats that require a longer cooking time. If you use a gas grill, preheat it until it reaches a temperature of 500°F to 550°F. For charcoal, count on a half hour of pre-grilling prep time; you want your coals to be ash gray.

Veal				
Chop	$3/4$	Medium-hot	Well-done	10 to 12
Lamb				
Chop	1	Medium	Rare	10 to 14
	1	Medium	Medium	14 to 16
	1	Medium	Well-done	16 to 20
Pork				
Blade steak	$1/2$	Medium-hot	Well-done	10 to 12
Canadian-style bacon	$1/4$	Medium-hot	Heated	3 to 5
Chop	$3/4$	Medium-hot	Well-done	12 to 14
	$1 1/2$	Medium	Well-done	35 to 45
Ham slice	1	Medium-hot	Heated	20 to 25
Miscellaneous				
Bratwurst		Medium-hot	Well-done	12 to 14
Hot Dog		Medium-hot	Heated	3 to 5
Ground meat patties	$1/4$ pound	Medium	Well-done	15 to 18

Indirect Grilling: Meat

Cut	Weight (pounds)	Doneness	Time (hours)
Beef			
Rolled rump roast	4 to 6	150° to 170°	$1^1/_4$ to $2^1/_2$
Boneless sirloin roast	4 to 6	140° rare	$1^3/_4$ to $2^1/_4$
		160° medium	$2^1/_4$ to $2^3/_4$
		170° well-done	$2^1/_2$ to 3
Eye of the round roast	2 to 3	140° rare	1 to $1^1/_2$
		160° medium	$1^1/_2$ to 2
		170° well-done	2 to $2^1/_4$
Rib eye roast	4 to 6	140° rare	1 to $1^1/_2$
		160° medium	$1^1/_2$ to 2
		170° well-done	2 to $2^1/_4$
Rib roast	4 to 6	140° rare	$2^1/_4$ to $2^3/_4$
		160° medium	$2^3/_4$ to $3^1/_4$
		170° well-done	$3^1/_4$ to $3^3/_4$
Tenderloin roast			
Half	2 to 3	140° rare	$^3/_4$ to 1
Whole	4 to 6	140° rare	$1^1/_4$ to $1^1/_2$
Top round roast	4 to 6	140° to 170°	1 to 2
Veal			
Boneless rolled (breast	2 to 3	170° well-done	$1^3/_4$ to 2
or shoulder) roast	3 to 5	170° well-done	$2^1/_4$ to $2^3/_4$

Loin roast	3 to 5	170° well-done	$2^1/_4$ to $2^3/_4$
Rib roast	3 to 5	170° well-done	$2^1/_4$ to $2^3/_4$

Lamb

Boneless leg roast	4 to 7	160° medium	$2^1/_4$ to $2^3/_4$
Boneless rolled shoulder roast	2 to 3	160° medium	$1^3/_4$ to $2^1/_4$
Rib crown roast	3 to 4	140° rare	$3/_4$ to 1
		160° medium	$3/_4$ to 1
		170° well-done	1 to $1^1/_4$
Whole leg roast	5 to 7	140° rare	$1^3/_4$ to $2^1/_4$
		160° medium	$2^1/_4$ to $2^1/_2$
		170° well-done	$2^1/_2$ to 3

Pork
Boneless top loin roast:

Single loin	2 to 4	170° well-done	$1^1/_2$ to $2^1/_4$
Double loin, tied	3 to 5	170° well-done	$1^3/_4$ to 3
Ribs, spareribs	2 to 4	170° Well-done	1 to 2
Loin blade or sirloin roast	3 to 4	170° well-done	$1^1/_2$ to 3
Rib crown roast	4 to 6	170° well-done	$1^3/_4$ to 3
Tenderloin	$3/_4$ to 1	170° well-done	$1/_2$ to $3/_4$

Ham (fully cooked):

Boneless, half	4 to 6	140° heated	$1^1/_4$ to $2^1/_2$
Boneless, portion	3 to 4	140° heated	$1^1/_4$ to $2^1/_4$
Smoked picnic	5 to 8	140° heated	2 to 3

As you'll discover when you see the number of such recipes throughout this book, chicken is one of our favorites for the grill. It's inexpensive, low in fat—if you follow our suggestions when you grill it—and it's delicious, too.

A Tisket, a Packet, A Special Foil-made Basket

Throughout this book, you'll often see us refer to packet grilling. We include a special section on that method in Chapter 17, but it's also used in the preparation of many side dishes, such as those we tell you about in the vegetable chapter, Chapter 13. Regardless of the packet-making instructions given with the recipe, any method that serves the function of sealing up the food so it will cook and steam will work. The three most common packet styles are:

1. **Rectangle Wrap:** Place your food in an oblong piece of heavy duty aluminum foil that's long enough for you to fold it at the top and sides. Bring the sides up and over the top of the food and fold it down, using a series of locked or crimped folds. Fold the short ends to finish sealing the packet.

2. **Bundle Wrap:** Place the food in the center of a piece of aluminum foil large enough to allow you to bring all four corners up and over the food. Twist the corners together to form what is also sometimes referred to as a "puff packet," and then fold the foil over at the twist to seal the top. This method will allow you to sometimes use a smaller piece of foil,

You'll ensure more even cooking if you truss your bird. Just wrap some pre-soaked kite string (so it doesn't get too hot and ignite) around the legs and body. Pretty doesn't matter since you'll disgard the string once the poultry comes off the grill.

Direct Grilling: Poultry

NOTE: White meat grills slightly faster than does dark meat.

Type of Poultry	Weight	Grill	Time (minutes)
Broiler or fryer halves	$1^1/2$ pounds	Medium	40 to 50
Chicken breasts, boneless, skinless	4 to 5 ounces	Medium	15 to 18
Chicken thighs, boneless, skinless	2 to 3 ounces	Medium	8 to 12
Cornish game hens, halves	$3/4$ pound	Medium-hot	45 to 50
Turkey breast tenderloin steaks	4 to 6 ounces	Medium	12 to 15
Ground turkey or chicken, patties	$1/4$ pound	Medium-hot	15 to 18

Indirect Grilling: Poultry

Type of Poultry	Weight	Time (hours)
Chicken, whole broiler or fryer	$2^1/2$ to 3 pounds	$3/4$ to 1
	$3^1/2$ to 4 pounds	$1^1/2$ to $1^3/4$
	$4^1/2$ to 5 pounds	$1^3/4$ to 2
Chicken, whole roasting	5 to 6 pounds	$1^3/4$ to $2^1/2$
Cornish game hens	1 to $1^1/2$ pounds	$3/4$ to 1
Pheasant	2 to 3 pounds	1 to $1^1/2$
Quail	4 to 6 ounces	about $1/2$
Squab	12 to 14 ounces	$3/4$ to 1
Turkey (Unstuffed)	6 to 8 pounds	$1^3/4$ to $2^1/4$
	8 to 12 pounds	$2^1/2$ to $3^1/2$
	12 to 16 pounds	3 to 4
Turkey, boneless whole	4 to 6 pounds	$2^3/4$ to $3^1/2$
Turkey breast, whole	4 to 6 pounds	$1^3/4$ to $2^1/4$
	6 to 8 pounds	$2^1/4$ to $3^1/2$

but you must take special care to make certain it seals completely; you may need to crimp along the foil edges leading to twisted top to ensure a good seal.

3. **Covered aluminum pie plate:** This method works best for food you don't need to turn over during the grilling process. Place the food in an aluminum pie pan and, using a piece of aluminum foil, create a lid by placing the foil over the top of the pan and crimping it to the edges of the plate.

PLAN AHEAD

By now, you should appreciate that *The Lazy Way* is truly the efficient way. In the same manner that a few minutes spent honing your to-do list and choosing your wardrobe the night before can save you countless time the next day, some advance planning eases your work around the grill, too. To help you do just that, see the next chapter—Chapter 4—for advice and shortcuts. You'll be well on your way to earning that Ph.G.—Doctor of Grillosophy—by the time you do.

Getting Time on Your Side

	The Old Way	The Lazy Way
Rushed trip to the store to buy what you need	45 minutes	0 minutes
Another trip to the store to buy what you forgot to get on the first trip	30 minutes	0 minutes
Added cooking time caused by lifting the grill lid	60 minutes	0 to 15 minutes
Stitching poultry to truss it versus *The Lazy Way* wrap method	15 minutes	5 minutes
Time needed to ignite damp charcoal	15 minutes	0 minutes
Time to lounge in the hammock	0 minutes	15 minutes or more!

Chapter four

Sanity-Saving Shortcuts and Tried 'n' True Tips

Y ou've heard the phrase, "Plan your work and then work your plan." It certainly can apply to grilling. You see, by spending a little bit of time now learning some planning tips and shortcut suggestions, what takes a bit of time and effort to put into practice will fast become habit, and soon you'll be grilling quickly and efficiently.

In this chapter, the valuable pre-planning information will include details on how to build and maintain a proper fire, smoking hints, and wood choice recommendations. We'll also cover grilling temperatures and safety matters as well.

THE "DON'T PANIC" PLANNING STAGE

Until you reach the enlightened state where you can intuit your next menu based on your psychic knowledge of what lurks at the back of your refrigerator, following these suggestions will help.

- Take baby steps at first. Don't feel obligated to use all new recipes for your entire meal. Pick one new one and serve tried 'n' true family favorites to go with it.

- Consider the inventory of food you already have on hand when picking out which recipe to try next. The task seems less daunting when you don't have to worry about stretching the grocery budget to learn a new skill.

- When you have leftovers in the refrigerator, consider how they can be adapted for use with your meal. We give you a few suggestions on doing just that later on in this chapter.

- When you need to plan an entire meal, first select your main course. Once you've decided on that, it's much easier to plan what else you need to go with it.

- Whether you're considering a week's worth of menus or one meal, remember that diversity is important. You create interesting contrasts when you vary the colors, flavors, textures, and temperatures of your meals.

- Adjust your menu according to the time of year. Serve cold soups (such as those suggested in Chapter 17) in the summer and heartier main dishes in the fall. Plan the vegetable and dessert portion of the meal based on the season, too.

- Be realistic about how much time you'll need to fix the meal you want and plan accordingly. If your first

YOU'LL THANK YOURSELF LATER

If the bees are a'buzzin' around your picnic table, give everyone a glass for their beverage instead of drinking from a can. The extra dishes or disposable products are well worth it when you consider you're helping your guests avoid swallowing (or worse, getting stung by!) an insect.

choice is so complex that it requires more time than you can allot to prepare it, adjust the menu. Food just doesn't taste as good if you lose your sanity in the process of preparing it.

THE QUEST FOR FIRE!

If you're using a gas grill, your task is a simple one. You only need turn on the fuel supply and punch the automatic starter or, in primitive cases, strike a match (or flick your grill-lightin' Bic). An electric grill is even simpler: Make sure it's plugged in, then turn it to ON.

If you plan to use charcoal, briquettes need a bit of coaxing to get them ready. You can use any of these methods to get them going:

Liquid Lighter Fluid: This is the most commonly used fire starter. Arrange the briquettes in a pyramid shape, then pour the fluid over them and let it soak in according to the directions on the label. Carefully ignite with a match.

Cube Starters: These premeasured, solid starters free you from the guesswork of how much liquid fluid to use. Arrange the briquettes in a pyramid above the cube starter, leaving a corner of the cube exposed. Then carefully ignite the cube.

Quick Lighting Charcoal: This is charcoal that has been pretreated with lighter fluid. You simply arrange the briquettes into a pyramid shape and ignite them.

Chimney Lighter: This is a tall cylinder with a metal grate at the bottom for air circulation. To use, you first remove the grill rack, place the chimney lighter inside, and fill it

A COMPLETE WASTE OF TIME

The 3 Worst Things to Do with Lighter Fluid:

1. Use gasoline instead of liquid lighter fluid intended for charcoal. The idea is to ignite the charcoal, not the neighborhood.

2. Add liquid lighter fluid after you've already started your fire. (See No. 1 above for the reason why.)

3. Fail to allow enough time for your coals to get ready. You not only want to bring the coals to temperature, you also want to burn off any starter fluid. Plan on setting the flame to the charcoal at least a half hour before you intend to place your food on the grill.

with briquettes. There's no need to use lighter fluid. Instead, place pieces of crumpled newspaper under the chimney, then place the chimney on the charcoal grate. Use a long match to ignite the newspaper through the holes in the chimney. When the coals are ready, carefully pour them onto the charcoal grate, being certain to use fireproof gloves and the other necessary safety equipment recommended by the fire starter manufacturer.

Electric starter: This is an electrical element that is placed under the coals for a few minutes. Make sure to check the manufacturer's instructions before using. In most cases, you must remove the element within 10 minutes or risk damaging it.

NOW YOU'RE SMOKIN'

Just because you're using a grill doesn't mean you can't enhance the smoke flavor. (For full-force smoker suggestions, see the internal grill accessories section in Chapter 2.)

Even without a grill designed specifically to be used as a smoker or without a smoker accessory, you can still enjoy true wood-smoke flavor. To adapt your grill so you too can enjoy the smoky goodness heretofore only experienced by those willing to spend the entire day slaving over a barbecue pit, follow these steps:

1. Soak your choice of wood chips in water for 30 minutes to an hour.

2. Follow the indirect grilling directions for positioning your coals given for your type of grill in Chapter 3, and place the wood chips on those coals.

YOU'LL THANK YOURSELF LATER

Conserve wood and still achieve that delicious smoky flavor. After you soak your wood pieces in water for an hour, wrap each one in a piece of foil. Use a pin to prick holes around the foil-wrapped wood and place on the coals according to the specifications for your grill. The wood will now last up to four times longer, or up to an hour.

3. Place food on the cooking grate according to the instructions for your grill. On a charcoal grill, you'll want to close the vents most of the way. Regardless of your grill type, cook with cover down, trying not to lift it more often than necessary. To take full benefit of using the wood chips, it's best to grill over a lower temperature and increase your grilling time.

4. Add additional wood chips every 15 minutes.

JUST WHICH WOOD WOULD A WOOD SMOKE CHOOSE IF A WOOD SMOKE COULD CHOOSE WOOD?

The type of wood you choose to enhance the flavor is just as important as the decision to add smoke in the first place. Each wood type has its own special flavor. You want to select the one that will enhance your entrée's essence, not distract from it. In some cases, mixing wood works. Once you've learned which smoke flavors you prefer, you can experiment to develop your own unique blends. For now, we recommend you use the woods with the foods listed in the table on the following page.

If you know a cabinetmaker or furniture craftsman who frequently uses your preferred choice of wood, such as cherry, ask him to save the sawdust for you. In addition to periodically tossing some sawdust directly on the coals, you can also soak some in water, form it into small blocks in a manner similar to making a mud pie, wrap that in foil, prick some holes in the foil, and then place the sawdust-filled foil packet on the coals.

QUICK 🔲 PAINLESS

To add smoke flavors to the food you grill, don't limit yourself to just wood. You can also soak herbs and use them to create smoke packets like the ones described for the sawdust.

Wood Recommendations

Use this wood...	If you're cooking...
Mesquite	Steak and other beef, lamb, chicken, turkey, other poultry
Hickory	Beef, chicken, pork, ribs, sausage
Cherry	Hamburger, turkey, chicken, lamb
Apple	Pork, beef, sausages
Peach	Salmon and other fish, beef, poultry
Pecan	Beef, chicken, sausage

Many grill chefs like to add water-soaked herb sprigs such as rosemary, thyme, oregano, and basil directly to the hot coals. Also try using dried herb packets (they resemble tea bags), custom-blended to enhance the flavor of meats, poultry, or seafood and available commercially. You can also use the actual tea that comes in tea bags, too. See Chapter 11 for instructions on how to use Earl Gray tea in a special spicy tea-smoke blend.

HOT ENOUGH FOR YOU?

As we've stated before, grilling is not an exact science. Still, you need to have an idea of your grill temperature in order to gauge how long to cook your foods so that they will be the best that they can be.

Some newer grills come with built-in temperature gauges. Otherwise, one way to judge the heat intensity of the coals is to carefully hold your hand, palm side down, about 6 inches above and over the area where you will grill the food. Start counting in a "one-one-thousand, ..." manner. When your hand feels too hot, withdraw it. The number of seconds you were able to hold your hand over the grilling area gives you a reasonably accurate idea about the coal temperature.

Refer to the table below for examples of direct cooking temperatures determined by this method.

For indirect cooking (see description in Chapter 3), the coals must be one level hotter to obtain the correct temperature over the drip pan. In other words, you'll need coals that register as having high heat to get medium-high heat over the pan.

Direct Cooking Temperatures

Number of Seconds	Coal Temperature
2	High
3	Medium-High
4	Medium
5	Medium-Low
6	Low

Flare-ups on the grill often occur when fat drips down onto the coals. To prevent flare-ups before they start, select leaner cuts of meat, or trim as much fat from the meat as possible.

SHOW YOUR COALS WHO'S BOSS!

If you need to control your coals to tone down the heat of your grill, try these cooling methods:

- Raise your grill rack
- Cover or close the lid to the grill
- Space the hot coals farther apart, using long-handled tongs
- Close the air vents halfway to restrict airflow to the coals
- On a gas or an electric grill, adjust the temperature setting

If you find that the coals aren't hot enough, try these techniques:

- Gently shake the grill or tap the coals with long-handled tongs to rid them of excess ash
- Lower the grill rack
- Nudge the coals closer together using long-handled tongs
- Add two or three briquettes to the hot coals
- Open the air vents so more air circulates
- On a gas or an electric grill, adjust the temperature setting

MEATY MATTERS

A primary goal when preparing meat is to cook it to the correct temperature to ensure you destroy any potentially harmful bacteria. Proper cooking has additional benefits as well: The meat is healthy and moist with better flavor.

Keep in mind that:

- Chicken is done when meat next to the bone is no longer pink. This will usually take 35–45 minutes if you're grilling chicken pieces; boneless, skinless chicken takes much less time to grill. Refer to the grilling charts in Chapter 3 to gauge the grilling time for whole chickens and other poultry.

- Lean beef remains juiciest if you only grill it until it's medium, which will show as pink in the center and gray around the edges when you cut into the steak.

- It's okay to leave pork so it's still a little pink in the center. If you overcook pork, it gets tough and has less flavor.

- If you're preparing it on an open grill (instead of inside of a packet), baste fish every few minutes with reserved marinade to keep it moist. Allow 4 to 6 minutes grilling time for each $1/2$-inch thickness. If fish is thicker than 1 inch, turn it once during cooking; otherwise, thinner pieces of less than an inch do not need to be turned.

Knowing in advance how meats are supposed to be cooked takes the guesswork out of grilling. With that knowledge, you can concentrate on preparing delicious meals, confident they'll be safe, healthy ones, too.

WHEN YOU HAVEN'T GOT ALL DAY

Employing a few shortcuts not only speeds up the grilling process, it lets you deposit the time saved back into your

QUICK ◼▥◼ PAINLESS

How ready is ready? Once ignited, regular charcoal briquettes usually take 20 to 30 minutes to burn hot enough to grill. When ready, the charcoal should appear ash gray in daylight or glow red at night.

Wine and beer aren't just for marinades, you know. (No, we're not talking about drinking them. How primitive!) Use one or the other instead of water to soak your wood chips or herbs.

day's account to use for other tasks. Pacing yourself is good advice. Here are some ways to do just that:

■ Defrost meat in the microwave, if necessary, before you grill. Otherwise, the outside of frozen meat will char while the interior remains too cold to destroy bacteria. (Just don't rush the defrosting process. Follow the instructions given for your microwave. Otherwise, if you use a temperature that's too high for too long, you run the risk of partially cooking the meat and making it tough.)

■ Precook foods such as poultry or ribs in the microwave or boil them the night before. Store them in the fridge until you are ready to grill, then use the grill briefly for that special "outdoors" flavor.

■ You can also precook vegetables. For example, boil ears of corn in water with some sugar added (1/4 cup per every 12 ears of corn) and then refrigerate the corn overnight. The next day, grill it until it's warm—a minute each side, or until your entrée is heated, too.

■ When preparing your marinade, don't panic if you find you're out of the type of sweetener called for in the recipe. Try substituting molasses, maple syrup, or honey instead.

Speaking of altering your "sugar" choices, let's take a look at our first recipe to give you an idea of what we mean.

Maple Teriyaki Chicken Quarters Backing

The amount of sugar you use in this marinade will depend on whether you use dry or sweet wine, or simply use Mirin (a Japanese sweetened white wine) and omit the sugar. Molasses instead of the maple syrup makes this marinade more robust and adds gusto. Try it with a tablespoon of honey or brown sugar instead, too.

Makes 8 Servings

$1/2$ to 1 teaspoon sugar

2 tablespoons white wine

2 tablespoons soy sauce

1 tablespoon toasted sesame oil

1 tablespoon lemon juice

1 clove garlic

2 scallions

1 tablespoon maple syrup

Optional: 4 teaspoons sesame seeds

1   In a glass bowl, dissolve sugar into the wine. (Heat for a few seconds in the microwave if necessary.) Stir in the soy sauce, sesame oil, and lemon juice and mix well.

2   Add the crushed garlic, finely chopped scallions, and maple syrup or your choice of sweetener and stir again. Add the sesame seeds if you choose.

3   This recipe makes enough for 8 boneless, skinless chicken thighs, or enough for 8 people if you serve each thigh over a generous portion of seasoned, fried rice. Otherwise, allow 2 thighs per person.

QUICK 🔲 PAINLESS

Substitute $1/4$ teaspoon each of roasted onion and sautéed garlic bases from Minor's for the crushed garlic and scallions. We've also used chicken base to create a sweetened broth instead of the wine. See Appendix A for information on bases from Minor's and Redi-Base.

Serving Sizes

If you're grilling...	Allow...
Boneless cuts of meat	4 to 6 ounces per serving
Bone-in cuts of meat	6 to 8 ounces per serving
Vegetables	$^3/_4$ cup (4 to 5 ounces) per serving

Now that you've decided *what* to cook, you need to determine *how much* to cook. Consult the table above.

INFUSE AN OIL YOU CAN'T REFUSE

Think of an infused oil as one in which *something* has been marinated to impart flavor. Infusing is the process. A resulting subtle, yet distinct, new flavor is the benefit.

To give you an idea of the possibilities, here is just one variety of infused oil. We use fresh herbs in this one; you'll notice throughout this book, that unless it states "fresh" in the recipe, we give the amounts for dried herbs—usually a third of what you'd use of the fresh. This one also makes an excellent basting sauce for grilled fish.

Makes 2 cups

2 cups olive oil
1 tablespoon lemon juice
Peel from $^1/_4$ of 1 lemon
3 cloves garlic
$^1/_2$ cup fresh basil
$^1/_4$ cup fresh parsley

IF YOU'RE SO
INCLINED

Instead of getting stuck in that same ol', same ol' butter-and-jelly rut for the dinner rolls, impress your friends by providing small bowls of honey or herb butters or containers of infused oil.

1. In a glass bowl or jar, combine the olive oil and lemon juice.

2. Grate the lemon peel and crush the garlic cloves. Chop the basil and parsley. Add to bowl.

3. Allow the mixture to stand at room temperature for 2 hours.

4. If you plan to store leftover oil, strain it through cheesecloth. The oil will keep for several days in the refrigerator. Place it on the table in a bottle or in dipping bowls. If used as a basting sauce, brush the fish with the oil when grilling.

SENSIBLE SUBSTITUTES

Once you learn to improvise (and go with the flow), you'll no longer panic when you discover you don't have a desired ingredient on hand. For example: Out of sour cream? Don't panic! Instead, you can mix together one of these substitutes:

- Blend 1 cup of cottage cheese with 1/3 cup of buttermilk or milk and 1 tablespoon lemon juice

- Blend equal parts cottage cheese and plain yogurt

- Blend 1 cup of cottage cheese with 2 tablespoons of lemon juice, 2 tablespoons of mayonnaise, and 1/4 cup of buttermilk

SECOND TIME AROUND REBOUND

Serving leftovers in one of these ways will make your family think you intentionally cooked extra the night before, if they even notice they're getting reruns.

QUICK ▦ PAINLESS

Use the bases and concentrates in Appendix A to create a wide variety of infused oil. In most cases, simply add 1/4 teaspoon of base concentrate (such as ancho pepper) to 1/3 cup olive oil, 1 tablespoon of fresh lemon juice, and 1 tablespoon of water.

- Serve thinly-sliced chicken breast, pork or other meat atop a bowl of Asian noodles, sprinkled with chopped cilantro and green onion, and a dash or two of toasted sesame oil.
- Cut extra corn off of the cob and add it to salsa.
- Add grilled shrimp to almost any main dish salad.
- Thinly slice leftover grilled pork or beef and layer it on toasted French roll sandwiches along with roasted peppers and sautéed onion.
- Mix leftover meatloaf with some vegetables and cheese, roll everything up in a tortilla shell, and toast on the grill.

SUSPECT GRILLING: GOOD CHOP/BAD CHOP

Last, but by no means least, in your quest to serve your friends and family (and yourself!) delicious meals, rest assured that you can do so and still make healthy food. Here are some recommendations to follow before you grill and while you are grilling.

Before You Step Up to the Grill

- If you use a bowl or pan to marinate foods instead of a plastic bag, be sure it's made of a noncorrosive material (glass, ceramic with a lead-free glaze, or stainless steel) that won't be affected by the acid in the marinade.
- To avoid contamination, never let the marinade in which you've soaked raw meat, fish, or poultry (or

IF YOU'RE SO
INCLINED

An easy way to achieve smoke flavor is to place food in an aluminum envelope padded with a layer of wood chips and sugar, such as The Food Smoker Bag from iSi North America, Inc. See Appendix A for ordering instructions.

the dish it's been in) come in contact with cooked food you'll be eating. In other words, don't use the dish you use to carry the raw meat to the grill as your serving platter, unless you wash it first. Also, play it safe and either discard the marinade after using it, or, if you do intend to use some as a sauce at the table, reserve some before marinating the meat. If you forget and all of the marinade has been contaminated, boil it to destroy the bacteria introduced by the raw meat.

▪ If a recipe calls for basting with marinade, in most cases don't baste during the last 10 minutes of grilling; that allows enough time for the marinade to cook through.

▪ Don't marinate meat, poultry, or seafood longer than 30 minutes at room temperature. If the recipe calls for longer marinating, place in the refrigerator.

▪ Remember: the more acidic the marinade—the greater the percentage of vinegar, lemon juice, or yogurt—the less time needed to marinate. Leaving meat or seafood in a highly acidic marinade for too long can alter the texture of the food and leave it unpleasantly mushy.

▪ Marinades only penetrate about $1/2$ inch (from all sides), so don't expect really thick cuts of meat to pick up flavor in the center.

▪ Unless you plan to slow-roast them on the grill, precook ribs, thick cuts of meat, and whole turkeys indoors before grilling. Then only sear them briefly

A COMPLETE WASTE OF TIME

The 3 Worst Things to Do Before You Grill Meat:

1. Thaw meat in the microwave on high. Follow the thawing instructions in your microwave owner's manual to ensure the best setting for your appliance.

2. Consider it cheating to use the microwave when you're in a hurry.

3. Spend so much time fretting about getting your meal to come out perfectly that grilling becomes a chore and is no longer fun.

over high heat, just long enough to caramelize the outside.

- To prevent food poisoning, keep foods chilled until you're ready to grill or serve them.

At the Grill

Only use extremely high temperatures to sear the food. Charring meat can produce chemical substances that have been shown to cause cancer in some animal studies. And when meat is browned with intense heat over a direct flame and fat drips on the fire and coals, it creates smoke containing carcinogens called polycyclic aromatic hydrocarbons. Following these suggestions will keep the grill from flaring up.

- If meat does char or burn, cut away the blackened portion.

- Raising the adjustable cooking racks to their highest position above the heat will help prevent charring.

- Brush barbecue sauces and glazes on only during last several minutes of grilling so they don't splatter and drip down on the flames; otherwise, the sugar in them can cause flare-ups and the wrong kind of smoke.

- Skimping on fat isn't always a good thing. In order to prevent charring, it's okay to leave fat on the meat to help it absorb the good smoky flavor and tenderize the meat as it melts. (Most of it melts away and is burnt off anyhow, so it doesn't end up on your plate or your hips!)

- Keep a squirt gun or bottle close by to put out unwanted grill flare-ups. Even when you take all of the precautions, unwanted flames can still occur.

- Lower the fat content of ground meats by mixing with rice, bread crumbs, crackers, or oatmeal before you shape it into patties. This suggestion also helps you stretch your main course when unexpected guests drop by. (Families are like that!)

- In the event of a hard-to-control flame, invest in a fifty-cent fire extinguisher and keep it near the grill. Fifty-cent fire extinguisher? Yep—a box of baking soda! Be careful not to get any on the food, since it'll raise the sodium content and distort the food's intended flavor. Aside from that, it's the cheapest and best prevention you can have on hand when a cut of meat turns out to be fattier, and flame-ier, than you anticipated.

Before ending this chapter, we want to share what we believe is our most important suggestion:

Enlist family and friends to help. It's our opinion that martyrs don't have as much fun.

YOU'LL THANK YOURSELF LATER

You wear an apron to protect your clothes. Always remember to wear clothes that protect *you*. The grill area is not the place to wear shirts with long, loose sleeves or a flowing scarf around your neck. Wind and flare-ups are unpredictable. You don't want your clothes (or long hair you forgot to tie back, for that matter) to get caught in the crossfire, so to speak.

Getting Time on Your Side

	The Old Way	**The Lazy Way**
Trimming the excess fat from meat	0 minutes	5 minutes
Time spent battling subsequent flare-ups	Continuously	Seldom
Checking the available fuel supply (charcoal or keeping a spare tank of gas)	0 minutes	1 minute
Time spent lighting the grill	45 minutes (includes a trip to pick up more charcoal or refill the gas cylinder)	2 minutes (with 13 to 28 minutes left over to relax while the grill preheats)
Time spent preparing side dishes	45 minutes (includes the trip to the deli and extra time to "doctor" your purchases so they look homemade)	15 minutes (making them the night before, so they're ready and waiting in the refrigerator)
Time spent fretting	30 to 60 minutes (the entire cooking and dining period)	5 minutes (nobody's perfect)

Minimizing the Mess

Where is it written that you have to prepare your sauce, marinade, relish, salsa, or side dish at the exact same time you intend to serve or use it? As a matter of fact, there are some benefits to advance preparation.

One, there's this synergy thing that occurs. After hanging around in the same mixture for a while, the ingredients all decide they're ready to cooperate and work together. We think they wrap their arms around each other's shoulders and maybe even choreograph some high kicks when our backs are turned. Whatever it is they do, hours later or by the next day when you need 'em, they've melded into a working unit, all the more delicious for having done so.

Two, and best of all, while they're doing their thing, they're also indirectly making your cleanup tasks a bit easier. When it's convenient, any work done ahead of time—inside and close to the sink—means you can clean as you go instead of creating one huge mess to deal with later.

Only you and the circumstances regarding each outdoor cooking event can determine whether it's more efficient to do some of your preparation steps inside near your stove and microwave or outside at the grill. Therein lies the first step in determining how to, as this chapter title suggests, minimize the mess.

Inside, as we've already indicated, you can keep dishwater ready for some cleanup details and, of course, the dishwasher is close by for others. Outside, it doesn't matter as much if you splatter a bit.

It's now time for you to decide which of *The Lazy Way* tips will work best for you. In addition to those we mention throughout the book, we've rounded up some others and placed them here—somewhat grouped together by function, but by no means listed in any order of importance. You don't have to adopt them all at once. Just keep in mind that although you may now dread a new cleanup routine because you have to stop and think about it, it will become a habit before you know it!

As you'll soon discover, making cleanup a breeze doesn't mean you wait for the wind to blow away the debris.

GROOMING THE GRILL

After the coals have burned down or, if you're using a gas or electric grill, after you've left the heat on for an additional few minutes following the cooking time, use a grill-grooming tool (a spatula-looking affair with wire rack-sized cutouts) or a wire grill brush to loosen stuck-on food particles.

A COMPLETE WASTE OF TIME

The 3 Worst Things to Do to Save Cleanup Time:

1. Forget to make it easy for everybody to recycle. Always keep separate containers for aluminum cans and trash close by.

2. Fail to use recycled paper products.

3. Become overwhelmed by the behavior changes we recommend.

For those times when the food left behind decides to be stubborn and therefore calls for more desperate measures, you can do one of the following:

1. Spray the grate with oven cleaner and rinse thoroughly.

2. Wash with hot soapy water and rinse well.

3. Use our preferred method of applying a paste made from baking soda and water. This method takes a bit longer, but you don't have to hover over the rack during the entire process. Apply the paste and go do something else for a while. If you notice that the paste is drying out before you're ready to scrub it a bit with your wire brush, simply moisten it by spritzing on some of that water you keep close by in a spray bottle to control flare-ups. Once you do scrub the rack, rinse thoroughly.

After you've cleaned your grill rack, remember that you need to "season" it before you use it again. This is best done after you've preheated the grill a bit, but if you do so, use appropriate safety measures to protect your hands and arms. Before you place food on the grill, rub the grid with vegetable oil or spray with non-stick cooking spray. This helps to prevent food from sticking, which means it'll be a long time before you have to wash and scrub the grid again.

You can line the grill box of your charcoal grill with aluminum foil for easy cleanup; fold the foil up and over the mess and dispose of it and voilà—you're ready to store the grill until its next use.

QUICK 💿 PAINLESS

If you use Suggestion 2 or 3 to clean your rack, you can do so outside. Hose the rack down when you're done, return it to the grill, and let it drip dry. You don't have to worry about children or pets coming into contact with this kind of cleaner residue.

Packet meals also minimize the mess, because the food you're grilling is tucked away inside aluminum foil. See Chapter 3 for tips on how to prepare a packet; Chapter 17 includes packet meal suggestions.

Some grilling accessories (such as griddles and woks) and utensils are coated with non-stick material for easy clean-up. Be sure to follow the manufacturer's instructions when using such products. Most nonstick-coated pans require that you use plastic utensils.

Otherwise, you'll save cleanup time if you "season" your grill-safe pans and iron skillets. After each cleaning, and before you add your food, preheat the pan over the grill, then lightly rub in some oil or spray on some non-stick cooking spray.

OTHER WAYS TO SAVE YOURSELF SOME TIME

That extra refrigerator you keep in the garage doesn't have to be limited to chilling your beer and soft drinks. Use it to store whatever condiments you plan to use with your grilled meals, too. That way the "fixin's" are always just a few steps away from the picnic table.

Scrape plates directly into the bag-lined trash containers you keep outside.

Use appropriately sized buckets and rubber tubs to transport the dirty dishes from the picnic table to the dishwasher or sink. This way everyone in the family can assist during cleanup and you don't have to worry that juices remaining on the plates will drip onto your clean floors.

Then, to clean up the transporting containers, have the kids carry them back outside and hose 'em down. Nowhere is it written that they have to be buffed and shined before you put them away. You can let them dry for a while in the sun. Or, hang them from their designated hooks or place them on their assigned shelf space in the garage and forget about them until next time. The world won't end if the humidity goes directly back into the atmosphere instead of getting there via a dish towel-wielding middleman.

Marinate your food inside of Zip-lock plastic bags. Simply add the marinade ingredients, then the meat, and zip to seal. Squish the bag all around so the marinade covers the meat. Then put the bag on a plate in the fridge and turn it occasionally to redistribute the marinade.

Why not sit in the sun while you clean those vegetables? Put the food in a colander and hose it down over your herb plants; this method washes the veggies and instantly recycles the water into the garden. Carry the colander back to the picnic table, put your feet up, and do your thing.

Create serving presentations that perform the dual duty of looking nice and reducing the amount of cleanup required. In a basket or on a tray, nestle filled (and disposable) salsa containers in between multi-colored paper napkins. At the end of the meal, just toss the contents of the basket or tray. Plus, the napkins serve the added function of catching drips and dribbles as your family or guests dip out their condiment portions.

IF YOU'RE SO
INCLINED

Another way to minimize the mess inside of your grill and save yourself some cleanup time is to use a disposable drip pan to catch juices from the food. This keeps your charcoal grill clean and, when you arrange the coals around the drip pan, it reduces flare-ups, too.

And last but not least, that container of pop-up pre-moistened towelettes isn't just for the baby's diaper bag. Keep one at the picnic table and one next to the grill.

Following these tips and coming up with a few of your own will simplify the cleanup process.

Now that you know *The Lazy Way* to handle the messes, let's start making them! The recipe chapters are next.

Sometimes having a few extra utensils to clean is worth it. Stop anyone from dipping into a condiment for a second helping with the same tortilla chip by placing a spoon inside each dip container. That way it's easy to transfer the condiments to each person's plate.

Getting Time on Your Side

	The Old Way	The Lazy Way
Doing the dishes	60 minutes (includes procrastination time and the time necessary to presoak the plates)	15 minutes (done at intervals, with a five-minute wrapup at the end that includes time enough to empty the dishwasher, buff the counters, and shine the faucets)
Handling the trash	30 minutes (includes time necessary to sort out the recyclables)	5 minutes (there's always somebody who doesn't clean up their own mess)
Cleaning the grill rack	60 minutes (carrying it inside, treating it with oven cleaner, finding your rubber gloves, airing out the room to remove cleaner fumes, scrubbing the rack and then rinsing it to remove all traces of the toxic cleaner, washing the rubber gloves, and washing toxic cleaner residue out of the sink)	5 minutes (since you first pre-treated it with nonstick spray, you can wash it with the recommended soda mixture, hose it down, and put it back on the grill to dry)

Part 3

The Flame Game: Recipes for Successful Grilled Meals

Are You Too Lazy to Read the Chapters on Recipes for Successful Grilled Meals?

1 Your family is convinced that the only entrée you know how to prepare is cold cereal. ☐ yes ☐ no

2 Your idea of a complex instruction is "add water." ☐ yes ☐ no

3 The closest you've come to grilling in a long time was when you forgot to take the tinfoil off the dish in the microwave. ☐ yes ☐ no

six

A Shiny New Coating

Many consider grilling to be an art unto itself. Others would disagree and call it a science. We tend to believe the former is more correct than the latter. Let's take a look and see if we can prove the point to you.

Artists use brushes; grill chefs do, too. Both dip their brushes into something and apply it to their "canvas." There is no scientific exactness in how a dish should taste. If you like it, that's when the dish has been created correctly. The same can be said for a painting. If you like what you see, the artist did a good job. See the similarities? No microscopes, beakers, or test tubes involved!

Take all of this into consideration while looking at the recipes in this book. They are here simply to provide you with information on (modestly speaking) masterpieces we've created. You can take that masterpiece and make it your own, depending on you and/or your family's individual tastes.

This chapter deals with the "paints" you'll be using to create your own works of art. We'll show you various rubs, marinades, and sauces to get you acquainted with some of the

Flavor-boosting a tender steak, fish, or poultry with a rub is ideal for those times you need to ready something for the grill in a hurry.

ingredients commonly used. Chapters 7 through 16 will have many more for you to look over, but for now we'll give you three or four each to get started. Try these and modify them if you wish. Remember, there's a da Vinci or Warhol hiding somewhere within you!

RUB-A-DUB-DUB, BUT NOT IN THE TUB

The least common method of seasoning meat for the occasional outdoor chef is the rub. Ironically, it's the easiest and most time-saving method of seasoning meat that's destined for the grill. Unlike a marinade, which includes some sort of acidic liquid such as vinegar or wine to tenderize the meat, a rub is all seasoning, all of the time.

There are two general types of rubs—dry and wet. Dry rubs are simply herb-and-spice mixtures that are spread thickly onto the meat and rubbed into the surface. Wet rubs are basically the same, except the herbs and spices are bound together with some sort of liquid, usually oil. Let's look at some recipes for use with various types of meat.

Deep-South Barbecue Rub

This is an excellent all-around beef rub. It can be used for pork, but it's much better on beef.

1 tablespoon brown sugar

1 tablespoon sugar

1 tablespoon chili powder

1 tablespoon ground cumin

2 tablespoons paprika

1 tablespoon salt

1 tablespoon freshly ground black pepper

1 teaspoon cayenne pepper

1 Mix all ingredients well.

2 Rub mixture into meat. Place meat in plastic bag and let sit for at least 2 hours.

3 Cook meat until done.

YOU'LL THANK YOURSELF LATER

Make sure you have extra amounts of the ingredients handy. The amounts listed in this chapter are only approximate, in comparison to the amount of meat you intend to cook. If you didn't create enough rub for your dish, simply add more amounts of the ingredients to compensate.

Place meat on top of a sheet of aluminum foil before you sprinkle on the dry rub. It'll keep your counter clean and after you transfer the entrée to the grill, you can simply fold up the foil and throw it away.

Firehouse Dry Rub

Can you say "hot?" Good. Have plenty of beverages handy while serving any dish using this rub. (And remember that this is a "dry" rub—the lemon juice goes directly on the meat, not in with the spices.)

$1/2$ cup lemon juice

5 ounces chili powder (about 2 spice rack-sized jars)

$1/2$ tablespoon cayenne pepper

2 tablespoons garlic powder

1 tablespoon black pepper

1 Coat all surfaces of the meat with lemon juice.

2 Mix all dry ingredients in a glass container. Sprinkle generously over the meat and rub in well, making sure entire surface of the meat is covered thoroughly.

3 Leftover rub can be sealed in the glass container and stored in the refrigerator.

Everything But the Kitchen Sink Rub

Here's a rub with lots of ingredients, but trust us, it's well worth every one of them! Try this on beef, pork, and poultry.

$2^1/_3$ tablespoons chili powder

$1^1/_3$ tablespoon paprika

$^1/_2$ teaspoon cayenne

2 teaspoons dried oregano

$^1/_2$ teaspoon black pepper

$^1/_4$ teaspoon thyme

$^1/_2$ teaspoon sugar

$^1/_4$ teaspoon tarragon

$^1/_2$ teaspoon dry mustard

$^1/_4$ teaspoon salt

$^1/_2$ teaspoon ground cloves

$^1/_2$ teaspoon celery seed

2 crushed bay leaves

$^1/_2$ teaspoon garlic powder

1 Mix all ingredients well.

2 Sprinkle over meat, rubbing in well.

QUICK 🔵 PAINLESS

While you're at it, go ahead and mix up a double batch of Everything But the Kitchen Sink Rub. You can store dry rub leftovers (that haven't come into contact with the meat) indefinitely in a covered glass jar.

Chicken à la Rub

This rub is an absolute "must try." It goes so well with chicken, there's no reason to try it with anything else.

1 tablespoon dried minced onion

1 tablespoon onion powder

$^1/_2$ cup onion

$^1/_4$ cup fresh chives

1 teaspoon coarse black pepper

$^3/_4$ teaspoon cayenne pepper

2 teaspoons dried thyme

$^1/_2$ teaspoon salt

1 teaspoon ground allspice

4 tablespoons lime juice

$^1/_4$ teaspoon ground nutmeg

2 teaspoons hot pepper sauce

$^1/_4$ teaspoon ground cinnamon

2 teaspoons sugar

Optional: 1 tablespoon oil

1. In a blender or food processor, combine all ingredients. Blend to a thick paste. (For skinless chicken, add the oil to the paste.)

2. Rub the paste thoroughly over the chicken, cover and refrigerate overnight.

3. Grill the chicken, without removing the paste before cooking.

YOU'LL THANK YOURSELF LATER

Never use the same dish that held the raw chicken as your serving platter without washing it first. Also, don't let any of the utensils that came in contact with the raw chicken touch the finished meat. Think "food safety first" at all times.

Gooey Garlic Rub

With or without the cayenne, this rub is delicious on pork tenderloin.

5 cloves garlic

1 tablespoon fresh parsley

1 teaspoon cayenne

$^1/_4$ cup olive oil

1 In a sealable plastic container, crush garlic and mix with parsley and cayenne.

2 Add oil slowly while mixing.

3 Seal and store in refrigerator until ready to use.

IF YOU'RE SO
INCLINED

See Appendix A, "How to Get Someone Else to Do It," for information on ready-to-use broth bases that can substitute for the oil in a wet rub. They save you some time on those days when you need to closely budget every moment.

IF YOU'RE SO
INCLINED

You can easily create your own ginger paste for the Ginger and Fish Marinade. Buy $1/2$ pound of ginger root and wash thoroughly. Chop and place in a blender with a small amount of water and cooking oil. Blend until a paste forms. If the mixture isn't smooth, add equal amounts of water and oil until it reaches the consistency of tooth-paste. Store leftover paste in an airtight container and refrigerate until ready to use.

Oh So Tangy Mustard Rub

Tangy and delicious describes any dish created with this rub.
Try it with a roast or a London broil.

> 1 bunch fresh parsley
> 2 cups Dijon mustard
> $1/2$ cup dried orange or lemon peel
> $1/2$ cup rosemary leaves
> $1/4$ cup black pepper

1 Mince parsley to fill 1 cup.

2 In a sealable plastic container, mix all ingredients.

3 Seal and refrigerate until ready to use.

MARINADES: IT WAS THE BASTE OF THYMES...

Marinades are liquids with seasonings added for flavor. They also usually contain an ingredient which is high in acidic content that helps to tenderize the meat which is being marinated. Try some of the recipes below to discover some unique tastes you can create from simple, and some not-so-simple, ingredients sitting in your cupboard now. Be sure to look at the end of this chapter for some tips and a marinade time guide to help you along the way.

Ginger and Lemon Fish Marinade

This goes so well with fish, we decided to put it in the title! However, you can try it on pork chops, too.

   4 tablespoons butter

   $1/2$ cup lemon juice

   2 teaspoons crushed garlic

   2 teaspoons ginger paste

   2 teaspoons Worcestershire sauce

   4 shakes Tabasco sauce—or to taste

1 In a small saucepan, combine ingredients. Stir until butter is melted.

2 Pour mixture over fish or pork chops, reserving a portion for basting. Let sit, refrigerated, for 30 minutes.

3 While cooking, baste with sauce every time you turn.

QUICK ☜☞ PAINLESS

To save yourself some time, place all of the ingredients in a microwavable container and zap it for about 1 minute, or until butter is melted.

If you have a "tender" mouth, you may want to substitute another pepper for the Habaneros. This pepper is one of the hottest in the world—be fore-warned!

Jamaican Jerk Marinade

Whether you use it on chicken or pork, this marinade will impress everyone sitting around your table.

1 bunch scallions

Piece fresh ginger root

1 onion

1 teaspoon salt

4 teaspoons Jamaican pimento or allspice

1 teaspoon nutmeg

1 teaspoon cinnamon

6 Habanero chiles

1 teaspoon black pepper

4 garlic cloves

2 tablespoons lime juice

$1/4$ cup olive oil

$1/2$ cup red wine vinegar

4 tablespoons soy sauce

4 tablespoons dark rum

2 tablespoons brown sugar

2 tablespoons fresh thyme

1 Chop scallions to fill 1 cup.

2 Grate ginger root to make 2 tablespoons.

3 Liquefy all ingredients in a blender or food processor.

4 Marinate meat according to the guide at the end of this chapter.

All-Purpose Marinade

A marinade that goes well with anything. Got an old leather shoe handy?

2 cloves garlic

1^1/$_2$ cups salad oil

2 tablespoons dry mustard

^{3}/$_4$ cup soy sauce

^{1}/$_2$ cup wine vinegar

^{1}/$_4$ cup Worcestershire sauce

2^1/$_4$ teaspoons salt

1 tablespoon black pepper

1^1/$_2$ teaspoons dried parsley flakes

^{1}/$_3$ cup juice of a fresh lemon

1 Crush garlic and, in a glass container, combine all ingredients. Mix well.

2 Cover and refrigerate until ready to use.

QUICK  PAINLESS

Save some time on cleanup by marinating food in a large, zip-closure, plastic bag. These bags are great for large cuts of meat, pork chops, whole fish, etc. Remember to turn the bag occasionally to marinate each side evenly.

Quick and Easy Marinade

Here's a fun one. Okay, what we're going to do is tell you what's in it, but you decide how much, and what type of ingredients you want in it. We'll give you the first two amounts, the rest is up to you!

16 ounces Italian salad dressing

$^1/_4$ cup dried onions

2 different types of pepper (black, white, cayenne, other)

Fresh herbs of your choice (rosemary, thyme, cloves, other)

1 In a glass bowl, mix all ingredients well.

2 Pour over the meat and let sit at least an hour, or longer, depending on the meat. (See the chart at the end of this chapter.)

If your mixture doesn't cover the meat while marinating, you may add up to 16 ounces of water to the marinade mixture. This will save you time because you won't have to turn the meat over. Congratulations! Now you can watch your favorite soap.

The Lazy Way

Honey Dijon Herb Marinade

You must try this on beef steaks or a small London broil. The mustard and honey gives a unique taste to these meats!

1 cup dry white wine

$1/8$ cup white Worcestershire sauce

1 large clove garlic

1 bay leaf

1 pinch white pepper

$1/8$ cup honey

$1/4$ cup Dijon mustard

1 teaspoon dried oregano

$1/2$ teaspoon dried basil

1 In a glass bowl, mix all ingredients.

2 Place meat in bowl, cover, and refrigerate according to the chart at the end of this chapter.

QUICK ⊏▥⊐ PAINLESS

Try this Mexican Rub (from Redi-Base): $1/4$ cup salad oil, 2 teaspoons cayenne pepper, 1 table-spoon vegetable Redi-Base, 2 cloves garlic, 1 tablespoon cumin powder, 2 tablespoons mesquite smoke flavor. Combine ingredients in a glass bowl. Lightly rub on meat. Grill immediately.

OH! YOU SAUCY THING!

If you open your refrigerator, you will most likely find an old bottle of leftover barbecue sauce. Why use the same store-bought sauce over and over? Make your own! It's fresh and tastes so much better. There are more recipes in the following chapters.

Basic Beef Barbecue Sauce

A basic sauce for use with any beef cut. This is one you'll use often. Play around and change it to your taste if you want.

2 tablespoons olive oil

3 cloves garlic

4 tablespoons minced onion

14 ounces tomato sauce

1 small can tomato paste

1 teaspoon dry mustard

1 tablespoon brown sugar

2 tablespoons vinegar

1 tablespoon Worcestershire sauce

2 teaspoons cayenne

1 teaspoon ground pepper

1 In a saucepan, heat oil. Crush garlic and add to pan with onion. Cook until slightly brown.

2 Stir in all other ingredients.

3 Bring to a boil and reduce heat. Allow to simmer until it becomes thick.

4 Use on ribs or steaks.

Florida Citrus Barbecue Sauce

How about this? The citrus juices make this sauce wonderful!
Try this sauce on beef, pork, or poultry for a taste of the
Sunshine State's best.

1 tablespoon vegetable oil

1 large onion

1 tablespoon ground red chiles

$^1/_4$ teaspoon ground red pepper

1 Ancho chile

1 cup orange juice, fresh

$^1/_2$ cup lime juice, fresh

2 tablespoons sugar

2 tablespoons lemon juice, fresh

Fresh cilantro

1 teaspoon salt

1 Heat oil in a saucepan. Chop onion and add to pan with ground red chiles and ground red pepper.

2 Seed and finely chop Ancho chile and add to saucepan. Stir frequently, until onion is tender, 5 minutes.

3 Dice cilantro to make 1 tablespoon and add with remaining ingredients.

4 Bring to a boil and reduce heat to low. Simmer uncovered 10 minutes, stirring occasionally.

QUICK ◯ PAINLESS

If you wish, you may substitute bottled citrus juice in this sauce to save yourself some time. Fresh is better, of course, but we don't always have time to spare.

Southwest-Style Barbecue Sauce

Ready for a different taste (assuming you don't live in Arizona or New Mexico)? The Ancho and Pasilla chile powders gives this sauce a nice "change of pace" taste.

2 tablespoons unsalted butter

$^1/_2$ medium red onion

1 clove garlic

6 plum tomatoes

1 tablespoon Ancho chile powder

1 teaspoon Pasilla chile powder

$^1/_4$ cup catsup

2 tablespoons Dijon mustard

2 tablespoons dark brown sugar

1 tablespoon honey

1 teaspoon cayenne

1 tablespoon Worcestershire sauce

1 In a medium saucepan over medium heat, heat the butter. Dice the onion and garlic and add to pan. Sauté until translucent.

2 Coarsely chop the tomatoes and add to saucepan.

3 Simmer for 15 minutes. Add all other ingredients and simmer for an additional 20 minutes.

4 Puree the sauce mixture in a food processor, pour into a bowl, and allow to cool at room temperature.

5 Use immediately, or cover and refrigerate.

IF YOU'RE SO INCLINED

Southwest-Style Barbecue Sauce freezes well. Make up a double batch and ice some away to have on hand when you need it.

Jamaican Barbecue Sauce

We just can't stay out of the Caribbean, huh? The islands have some of the most wonderful sauces for barbecue. Here's another. This is a taste for the ages here. Don't worry about the rum in this sauce; remember, the alcohol burns off while cooking.

$^1/_2$ cup catsup

3 tablespoons soy sauce

2 tablespoons dark brown sugar

2 tablespoons distilled vinegar

1 piece fresh ginger

1 clove garlic

2 scallions

1 tablespoon dark rum

1 In a small saucepan, combine the catsup, soy sauce, brown sugar, and vinegar.

2 Mince ginger to make 1 tablespoon and add. Mince garlic and scallions and add.

3 Bring to a boil. Simmer over low heat until thick, 10 minutes.

4 Stir in the rum during the last 2 minutes.

A COMPLETE WASTE OF TIME

The 3 Worst Things to Do with Fresh Peppers:

1. Rub your eyes without washing your hands thoroughly.

2. Pop a handful into your mouth just for a taste.

3. Forget to wear gloves when cutting them up for a recipe.

HELPFUL MARINADE TIPS

Getting in *The Lazy Way* habit never involves cutting corners when it comes to taste, convenience, or safety. You've probably heard the line: "Support bacteria; it's the only culture some people have." However, humor, too, has its place. Maintaining cooking safety is the time to be serious. You certainly don't want cross-contaminations of foodstuffs to turn your marinade storage container into some sort of biohazardous petri dish. Following our suggestions will prevent that from happening—and help you create some awesome-tasting dishes, too.

- Marinades have a high acidic level. Therefore, always use a glass, ceramic, or stainless steel container in which to marinade your meats. NEVER use aluminum!

- A marinade should completely cover the meat. If it doesn't, turn the meat approximately every 2 hours to ensure evenly marinated meats.

- Always cover and refrigerate foods while marinating. Leaving marinating food at room temperature could allow the growth of bacteria in the marinade mixture, or on the meat itself.

- Beef roasts and other large cuts of meat are best if marinated for up to 2 days. The extra time allows the flavor to work its way into the center of the meat and helps tenderize it in the process.

- Thin or tender cuts can marinate according to a balance between the recipe instructions and your tastes, i.e., how much of the flavor you wish to impart to the meat.

- You can serve leftover marinade over cooked meats, but be sure to boil it for 5 minutes before using in this manner. This will kill any bacteria that may have formed in the liquid.

- NEVER baste food, while cooking, with marinade which hasn't been boiled as stated in the item above.

TIME TO APPRECIATE THAT WE'RE GONNA MARINATE GUIDE

When in doubt, get a second opinion. That's why we've put this Marinating Time Guide here for you. Bookmark the next page; you'll probably want to refer to it often.

YOU'LL THANK YOURSELF LATER

While we often recommend experimentation, we also strongly believe you must know the rules before you break them. Always follow marinating instructions the first time you try a recipe. Otherwise, it's hard to tell what you'll end up with.

Marinating Time Guide

Place in marinade...	Keep in marinade...
Fish Fillets	Up to 30 minutes
Fish Steaks	Up to 1 hour
Whole Fish	Overnight
Shrimp	Up to 30 minutes
Beef: Steaks	2 hours to overnight
Beef: Roasts	Up to 2 days
Pork: Chops	2 hours to overnight
Pork: Roasts	Overnight
Poultry: Breasts	1 hour to overnight
Poultry: Whole	Overnight

Getting Time on Your Side

	The Old Way	The Lazy Way
Creating a grilling work of art	60 minutes	5 minutes (the time it takes to search for this book and settle on your master-piece du jour)
Preparing dry rub per grilling session	10 minutes	5 minutes (since you now mix up a double batch and store some for later)
Preparing sauce to serve with the meat	30 minutes	5 minutes (the time it takes to boil leftover marinade to destroy bacteria)
Looking for marinating time suggestions	30 minutes	30 seconds (you did bookmark that page, right?)
Getting ready to have a hot time	60 minutes (includes a trip to the store to purchase some of that fake stuff made in—shudder—New York City)	10 minutes (mixing up one of the authen-tic spicy sauces in this chapter)

A Chicken on the Grill Is Worth Two in the Yard

We know, we know: Everything tastes like chicken! Why strap on the ol' hunting boots and the camouflage gear to drive across town to the exotic meats store for something that "tastes like chicken?" Why not eat the real thing? Besides, it's *chicken season* year-round everywhere! No license (or ammo) required.

It's up to you as to what kind of chicken you slap on your grill. You can purchase it *fresh* from the supermarket. Or, if you insist that your entrée first observed a fitness routine of running laps around the barnyard, check out the free-range varieties available at specialty markets or direct from the farmer. (If you only have a generic one on hand, yet still want to feel closer to nature, you could flex the chicken's legs into some stretching exercises before you cut it up.) Your call. We love 'em all!

In this chapter, you'll discover chicken recipes that are simple, tasty, and unforgettable. Ready that spatula or two-pronged fork and let's get with it.

Oriental Grilled Sesame Chicken

Grilled Sesame Chicken goes well with wild rice and salad, and has a certain Oriental quality. Another option is to serve it over a wide pasta, like fettuccine, covering it with leftover (and reserved to avoid cross-contamination) marinade.

Makes 4 to 6 servings

2 tablespoons sesame seeds

1 tablespoon sugar

$^1/_2$ cup soy sauce

$^1/_4$ cup water

$^1/_2$ cup vegetable or olive oil

1 teaspoon ground ginger

$^1/_8$ teaspoon ground red pepper

1 white onion

2 cloves garlic

4 chicken quarters or 6 chicken breasts

1 In large, non-metallic container, mix together sesame seeds, sugar, soy sauce, water, oil, ginger, and red pepper. Chop onion to make $^1/_4$ cup and add.

2 Mince the garlic and add to the above mixture.

3 Add chicken, cover tightly, and refrigerate at least 12 hours, turning occasionally.

4 Remove chicken from marinade and reserve liquid.

5 Grill 4 to 5 inches from medium-hot coals, turning and basting with reserved marinade frequently, for about 15 minutes total.

IF YOU'RE SO
INCLINED

For a change of pace, have a Peking picnic party. Get out those chopsticks and serve Oriental Grilled Sesame Chicken with fried rice, stir-fried vegetable salad, and fortune cookies for dessert.

w00h00 Worcestershire Chicken

This recipe is especially good if you allow the flames to flare up during cooking. The lightly charred chicken skin adds a distinct flavor, as does the smoke from the chicken fat that melts away and drips onto the coals.

Makes 4 servings

1 tablespoon cider vinegar

$1/8$ cup Worcestershire sauce

$1/8$ cup water

2 tablespoons butter

2 tablespoons honey

1 chicken, quartered

1 In a glass bowl, combine cider vinegar, Worcestershire sauce, water, butter, and honey, and heat over low flame or in the microwave until butter melts.

2 Place chicken on grill and baste often with the sauce.

3 Grill for 7 to 8 minutes per side or until juices from chicken run clear.

A COMPLETE WASTE OF TIME

The 3 Worst Things to Do with Salt:

1. Add salt to any of the recipes using soy or Worcestershire sauce. The sodium content in those sauces is sufficient to act as a flavor enhancer.

2. Use garlic salt as a substitute for minced garlic. You'll end up with a recipe far too high in sodium, and the flavor will suffer, too.

3. Forget to throw some over your shoulder for good luck if you spill any.

QUICK ⬤ PAINLESS

Hawaiian Grill Chicken Salad

This is a good all-purpose meal which is relatively quick to create and is diverse enough to impress friends and family alike. No grass skirts required here, so have fun with this one.

Makes 6 servings

2 tablespoons prepared mustard

$2/3$ cup unsweetened pineapple juice

3 tablespoons soy sauce

2 tablespoons red wine vinegar

1 tablespoon honey

$1^1/2$ pounds of chicken tenders

1 bunch leaf lettuce

One 14-ounce can pineapple tidbits

3 Anaheim (mild) peppers

1 small onion

$1/2$ cup almonds

$1/4$ cup sesame seeds

1 In saucepan, add mustard, then slowly stir in the pineapple juice to prevent lumping.

2 Add soy sauce, vinegar, and honey; place over high heat and bring to a boil.

3 Pour the warm sauce over chicken. Cover and refrigerate at least 1 hour.

4 Remove chicken from marinade. Place marinade in small saucepan and boil 3 minutes.

5 Place chicken on prepared grill about 6 inches from heat.

6 Grill, turning and basting with boiled marinade, about 6 minutes or until fork can be inserted in chicken with ease.

7 To assemble salad, arrange lettuce on a plate, then add pineapple.

8 Clean pepper and onion; slice both into rings and arrange on lettuce.

9 Toast the almonds and sesame seeds. Slice almonds and sprinkle with sesame seeds over salad.

10 Top with grilled chicken tenders and spoon remaining marinade over all.

IF YOU'RE SO
INCLINED

You can add a little variety to your salad by using a different pepper from time to time. Other peppers in the same "hotness" range include the Cherry, Guajillo, and Poblano varieties. For something hotter, try an Ancho or Chipotle type.

Grilled Honey-Mustard Chicken

Is it sweet because of the honey, or tangy because of the mustard? Hmmm. Kind of remind you of a beer commercial? You decide with this one! We know one thing for sure—it is absolutely delicious. Your mouth will thank you afterward. Serve over long-grained wild rice, with vegetable side dishes.

Makes 4 servings

To Make Honey-Mustard Dressing

$1/3$ cup mayonnaise

$3/4$ cup sour cream

$1/3$ cup prepared mustard

$1/3$ cup honey

1 tablespoon fresh lemon juice

Salt and pepper to taste

To Make Honey-Mustard Chicken

$1/4$ cup Honey-Mustard Dressing

3 heaping tablespoons stone-ground Dijon mustard

2 tablespoons lemon juice

1 tablespoon honey

Salt and freshly ground black pepper, to taste

4 boneless, skinless chicken breasts (about 4 ounces each)

1   To make dressing, mix mayonnaise, sour cream and mustard with wire whisk. Add honey, lemon juice, salt, and pepper, stirring until well combined.

2 In a large bowl, whisk $^1/_4$ cup of the Honey-Mustard dressing with the Dijon mustard, lemon juice, honey, salt, and black pepper.

3 Coat chicken halves in mixture. Cover and marinate 1 hour or overnight. Scrape excess marinade from chicken. Place chicken about 6 inches above medium-hot coals.

4 Grill chicken, turning occasionally, for 3 to 5 minutes per side until juices run clear.

IF YOU'RE SO INCLINED

You can serve Grilled Honey-Mustard Chicken, tossed with a pasta, as a green salad topped with honey-mustard dressing or as a main dish.

To Live for Chicken Marinade

Name brands are given in this recipe because each offers its own distinct flavor. Combining the variety of sauces is what gives Pam's original recipe its wonderful taste.

Makes 8 servings

1 clove garlic

1 tablespoon butter

1 tablespoon honey

$1/8$ cup La Choy soy sauce

$1/8$ cup Kikkoman soy sauce

$1/8$ cup French's Worcestershire sauce

$1/8$ cup Lea & Perrins Worcestershire sauce

8 boneless, skinless chicken thighs

1 Mince garlic and add it with the butter to a microwave-safe bowl. Sauté by microwaving on high for 15 to 30 seconds. Add remaining ingredients and whisk until thoroughly combined.

2 Coat chicken thighs with the marinade.

3 Grill over high heat with a flame. Once flame has seared the meat (which caramelizes the sugars in the sauce), lower heat to medium and grill for an additional 3 to 5 minutes, or until juices run clear.

Optional: Fresh rosemary complements the flavors in this marinade. For a change of pace, sprinkle some on the chicken while you grill it. You'll love the added aroma, too.

Trust Us on the Vinegar Chicken

This recipe brings back memories of childhood cookouts with chickens split in half, slowly sizzling on the huge grill dad had made out of a burn barrel. This sauce is best if used to baste the chicken often. The original recipe calls for pints of the ingredients; we've cut it down to "at home on the grill" sized proportions.

Makes 4 servings

$^1/_8$ cup cider vinegar

$^1/_8$ cup water

2 tablespoons butter

1 tablespoon Worcestershire sauce

1 whole chicken, quartered

1 In a glass dish, combine the cider vinegar, water, butter, and Worcestershire sauce and heat over a low flame or in the microwave until butter melts.

2 Place chicken on grill and baste with the sauce. Turn the chicken and baste often.

3 Grill chicken for about 10 to 15 minutes per side; it's done when juices run clear.

IF YOU'RE SO INCLINED

For an enhanced flavor, marinate the chicken for an hour in the refrigerator in half of the Trust Us on the Vinegar sauce. Use the reserved marinade to baste the chicken during grilling.

Caribbean Thyme Chicken

You ever have one of those days where you feel like grabbing a fistful of the seasonings you have on hand and seeing what you can come up with? Pam created this recipe for one of her Ohio mid-winter treks through the snow to use the gas grill.

Makes 6 to 8 servings

Dry Rub Seasoning Mix

$1/2$ teaspoon ground allspice

$1/2$ teaspoon ground nutmeg

$1/4$ teaspoon ground cinnamon

$1/2$ teaspoon ground clove

1 teaspoon ground thyme

$1/4$ teaspoon ground cayenne pepper

$1/4$ teaspoon ground garlic salt

$1/4$ teaspoon ground garlic powder

To Make Carribean Thyme Chicken

5 pounds skinned chicken pieces

Walnut or olive oil to coat

1 Combine ingredients for the dry rub.

2 Wash chicken and pat dry with paper towels. Lightly coat chicken pieces with walnut or olive oil.

3 Rub seasoning mixture into chicken pieces.

4 Grill over medium flame for 10 to 15 minutes per side. Chicken is done when juices run clear.

QUICK ❚❚ PAINLESS

Keep in mind that boneless chicken takes less grilling time. If you buy boneless chicken, you won't have to get your hands icky deboning it yourself and will have more time to choose the next recipe to try!

Orange You Glad You Made This Chicken

You'll need to grill this dish a little farther away from the flame and watch it closely so it doesn't scorch, but it's worth the extra effort. You'll savor this sweet and salty, succulent and stimulating taste sensation.

Makes 4 servings

1 garlic clove

$^1/8$ cup orange marmalade

1 tablespoon sherry

1 teaspoon red wine vinegar

2 teaspoons soy sauce

2 teaspoons honey

4 boneless, 4-ounce, skinless chicken breasts or thighs

1. Mince the garlic enough to make $^1/4$ teaspoon for use in the recipe. In a glass bowl, combine the garlic, orange marmalade, sherry, red wine vinegar, soy sauce, and honey, and mix well.

2. Coat chicken with mixture.

3. Grill over medium heat for 3 to 5 minutes each side or until juices run clear.

YOU'LL THANK YOURSELF LATER

To avoid contaminating any reserved marinade, try our two-fisted basting method:

1. Place dish of reserved marinade within easy reach on your grill shelf.

2. With one hand, use a spoon to drizzle on the marinade while you baste with the brush in your other hand.

3. When not basting, it's okay to leave the spoon in the marinade, but place the brush (which has touched the raw chicken) in a separate container.

4. When the chicken is almost done and you baste for the last time, use the back of the spoon to spread the marinade instead of the contaminated brush.

Tasty Tahini Chicken

This recipe has a slightly nutty flavor. If you prefer something a bit stronger or want to please the kids, substitute peanut butter for the Tahini. Prepared either way, it's sure to become a family favorite.

Makes 4 servings

1 clove garlic

1 teaspoon roasted Tahini paste

$1/4$ teaspoon toasted sesame oil

1 teaspoon candied ginger

1 teaspoon honey

1 teaspoon soy sauce

1 teaspoon Worcestershire sauce

Four 4-ounce boneless, skinless chicken breasts or 4 thighs

1 Mince garlic and add to Tahini paste and sesame oil in a glass bowl. Sauté in the microwave on high for 30 seconds.

2 Combine the above mixture with the chopped candied ginger, honey, soy sauce, and Worcestershire sauce.

3 Coat chicken and grill over medium to low heat, about 6 inches above the coals. (Watch chicken closely because it will scorch.) Grill chicken 3 to 5 minutes on each side or until juices run clear.

IF YOU'RE SO
INCLINED

Before you mix the ingredients for Tasty Tahini Chicken, consider:

1. **Wash 4 potatoes, pierce them, and microwave on high for 5 minutes.**

2. **Mix up a double batch of the Tasty Tahini Chicken sauce.**

3. **Slice the potatoes and coat with half of the sauce.**

4. **Grill the potatoes along with the chicken.**

Getting Time on Your Side

	The Old Way	The Lazy Way
Deboning chicken	30 minutes	0 minutes (when you buy flash-frozen skinless, boneless breasts or thighs)
Trips to the exotic meats store	60 minutes (includes time to don those fatigues)	0 minutes
Minutes spent daily listening to family members whine "chicken again?"	20 minutes (they're real complainers, aren't they?)	0 minutes (you now have so many ways to prepare it, they don't even notice you bought a month's supply on sale)
Wrapping up leftovers	10 minutes	0 minutes (although now your family is whining that you didn't grill enough)
Getting organized	60 minutes (on each 10 minute task)	5 minutes (to ready it all! You are picking up some good habits, aren't you?)
Lounging in the hammock	0 minutes	55 minutes

What's the Beef Here?

What's the first thing that pops into mind when you think "barbecue"? (Say "beef" here.) That's right! Beef! There's probably more recipes for beef than there are ways for a politician to get into trouble. However, here're a few to get you started.

You don't have to follow these exactly. The recipes in this chapter are "tried and true," so to speak. Try adding or removing ingredients of your liking or disliking. After all, a recipe isn't created in a day.

Get to know the man or woman in the white apron behind the the meat counter at your local market. That way, whenever you have a question about whether or not you can substitute one cut of beef for another, you have somebody whose opinion you know you can trust. Because, while pretty much any cut of beef can be prepared on the grill, special cuts often need special consideration. Some are too tender to marinate for very long; others are too tough to grill without special preparation first. We give you some suggestions throughout this chapter. Your "butcher" can give you instant advice.

Gulf Coast Hurricane Hamburgers

Keith created these burgers after one of two hurricanes in 1995. Lack of electrical power savagely forced cooking on the grill. In the maddening rush to salvage his frozen food, he quickly became Experimental Chef, soon to be hailed from all corners of...his yard. This was the best of the dishes—if some could be called that—made on that day.

Makes 8 servings

4 pounds ground beef, round or chuck

2 teaspoons garlic powder

1 tablespoon parsley, dried flakes or fresh

2 teaspoons Tony Chachere's Cajun Creole Seasoning

$1/2$ teaspoon pepper

$1^1/2$ cups of mesquite barbecue sauce

1 medium white onion

1   In a large bowl, mix ground beef, garlic powder, parsley, Creole seasoning, and pepper well. Form eight $1/2$-pound patties, 1 inch thick.

2   Grill patties over medium-high heat for 2 minutes, turn. Repeat. Add barbecue sauce in desired amount to patties and continue to grill the patties until done, 16 to 20 minutes, turning once or twice.

3   Slice peeled onions into $1/2$-inch slices. Break into rings. Grill the rings on grill-top for 5 minutes, turning once.

4   Serve, on buns, with choice of condiments and toppings.

Not-so-London(ish) Broil

Here's a friend's original recipe which goes well with baked potatoes and grilled garlic bread. One of Keith's favorite beef recipes, without a doubt.

Makes 6 to 8 servings

1 teaspoon Tony Chachere's Cajun Creole Seasoning

$^1/_2$ teaspoon meat tenderizer

$^1/_2$ teaspoon poultry seasoning

$^1/_2$ teaspoon garlic powder

2 teaspoons water

One 3- to 4-pound London broil ($1^1/_2$ to 2 inches thick)

2 teaspoons butter

Black pepper, to taste

1 In measuring cup with a spout, mix together Creole seasoning, meat tenderizer, poultry seasoning, garlic powder and water.

2 With a sharp knife, make a deep, blade-width entrance cut into the side of the meat, being careful not to puncture the opposite side of meat. Keeping the entrance cut as narrow as possible, slice the inside of meat, creating a pocket.

3 Pour seasoning mixture into narrow opening in the meat. Refrigerate for 2 hours.

4 Spread butter over top of meat. Add pepper, to taste. Place in aluminum foil or grilling bag. Seal tightly.

5 Place on grill and cook for 30 minutes. Turn, and cook until it reaches desired doneness. Slice into $^1/_4$- to $^1/_2$-inch-thick pieces to serve.

IF YOU'RE SO INCLINED

Even though this London broil is delicious as is, you can add other ingredients on top of the meat before closing the foil or bag to enhance the flavor further. Try:

- sliced mushrooms
- onions
- barbecue sauce

Marinate cheaper cuts overnight or even longer. (Pierce really tough cuts of meat with a fork first.) The vinegar will tenderize the meat.

Pucker Up Grilled Steak

Is it the steak, the cook, or the diners that are supposed to pucker up from this recipe? We were never able to decide which until we tried it. Try it to find out for yourself. (Hint: If you want the pucker less pronounced, ponder pouring red wine or beer into your marinade instead of the red wine vinegar.)

Makes 4 servings

1 clove garlic

1 tablespoon butter

$1/8$ cup soy sauce

$1/8$ cup red wine vinegar

$1/8$ cup catsup

2 tablespoons honey

Four 8-ounce steaks of choice

1   Mince garlic and add to butter in microwave-safe container. Microwave for 30 seconds, or until butter is melted.

2   Add soy sauce, red wine vinegar, catsup, and honey. Mix well.

3   Place steaks in shallow glass dish and pour marinade over the steaks. Refrigerate for 4 to 6 hours, covered.

4   Grill steaks over medium-high heat until cooked to desired doneness 20 minutes, turning once.

Beefy Caesar Salad

Want something quick and light as a snack, or even a side dish? A Caesar salad is always a good answer for the situation.

Makes 4 servings

1 tablespoon white wine vinegar

1 teaspoon Worcestershire sauce

1 pound sirloin stir-fry strips

Parmesan cheese

One 10-ounce bag prepared Romaine lettuce salad mix

1 cup croutons, Caesar flavored

1 tablespoon Dijon mustard

$^1/_3$ cup low-fat Caesar salad dressing

1 Mix vinegar with the Worcestershire sauce and pour over sirloin strips. Marinate for 30 to 40 minutes.

2 Heat cast-iron skillet on a hot grill and sear beef for one minute on each side. Thread strips onto skewers and grill for 4 to 6 minutes.

3 Shred $^1/_2$ cup cheese.

4 Place salad mix, croutons, and cheese into a large serving bowl. Add grilled strips of beef, cut to desired length.

5 Mix mustard with Caesar dressing and pour over salad. Toss and serve immediately.

QUICK PAINLESS

Avoid dropping the seared beef strips into the coals while you thread them onto the skewers. Place a piece of heavy-duty foil over the grilling area. Puncture the foil with a fork several times to allow the flavor of the smoke to penetrate through to the meat.

An easy way to build your fire on one side of a charcoal grill is to use two bricks in the middle—placed end-on-end—to halve the cooking area.

Grill-Roasted Beef and Pepper Dinner

If you like everything cooking in front of you at once, here's your answer. Your grill will sag from the weight of this great recipe.

Makes 4 servings

2 teaspoons ground black pepper

2 teaspoons garlic powder

1 teaspoon corn starch

$1/2$ teaspoon salt

Pinch each of ground thyme, white pepper, and cayenne pepper

$1^1/2$ to 2 pounds beef shoulder roast

4 medium baking or sweet potatoes

4 ears corn on the cob, unshucked

1 red bell pepper

1 green bell pepper

1   In a bowl, mix together black pepper, garlic powder, corn starch, salt, thyme, white pepper, and cayenne to make a rub. Press mixture into both sides of roast.

2   For conventional grills, build wood or charcoal fire to one side. Use enough fuel to sustain heat for 1 hour. For gas grills, preheat one side; turn to low.

3   Wash potatoes, pierce with a fork, and brush with oil.

4 Place beef, potatoes, and corn on cool side of grill. Cover and cook 50 to 60 minutes; maintain grill temperature of 300° F. De-seed and quarter peppers, add to hot side of grill and cook covered during last 10 minutes.

5 Check roast with meat thermometer inserted in center. Remove when thermometer reads 140°F for medium-rare or 155°F for medium. Let stand 10 minutes before carving, which allows the juices to redistribute throughout the meat. Slice thinly across the grain. Serve with peppers, potatoes, and corn. Use leftover sauce if desired. To serve corn, peel back husks.

YOU'LL THANK YOURSELF LATER

Cutting beef is one of the times you do want to go "against the grain." Slice it with the grain and you end up with a stringy and tough mess. Yuck! Portion it against the grain and you get pieces that are more tender and less chewy.

Calypso Caribbean Steak

Bring the taste of the islands to your table with this wonderful steak creation. Undo the top button on the ol' trousers and...do you hear them?...steel drums playing softly in the background as you eat....

Makes 4 to 6 servings

1 small onion

1 or 2 jalapeño peppers

3 cloves garlic

$^1/_4$ cup soy sauce

$^1/_4$ cup honey

$^1/_4$ cup lime juice

10 to 20 thin slices peeled fresh ginger

1 teaspoon whole brown mustard seeds, optional

$^1/_2$ teaspoon allspice

$^1/_2$ teaspoon paprika

$^1/_2$ teaspoon thyme

1$^1/_2$ pounds top round or top sirloin steak, 1-inch thick

1 Cut onion into chunks. Remove stems and seeds from jalapeños and cut in half. Peel garlic cloves.

2 Blend onion, soy sauce, honey, lime juice, ginger, jalapeño, garlic, mustard, allspice, paprika, and thyme in a blender or food processor until mixed well.

3 Place steak in a sealable plastic bag or shallow glass dish and pour marinade over steak. Seal well and refrigerate 20 minutes to 6 hours, turning bag, or steaks, occasionally. Remove meat, reserving marinade.

YOU'LL THANK YOURSELF LATER

Use rubber gloves when cutting hot peppers. Be careful not to rub your face, especially the eye area, before removing the gloves.

4 Grill steak 4 to 6 inches from medium coals for about 16 to 20 minutes, turning once, until done. Remove steak to carving board and let stand 10 minutes.

5 Bring reserved marinade to a boil in a saucepan over medium-high heat. Reduce heat and simmer for 3 to 4 minutes.

6 Carve steak into thin slices, diagonally. Place on a platter and cover with heated sauce.

QUICK ⬭ PAINLESS

Don't give bacteria a chance to party on your steaks before you grill 'em. Wait until the last possible moment to remove them from the refrigerator. Sure, they grill faster if they're at room temperature. (But which room, which season?) As long as they're not frozen solid, you'll be fine.

Louisiana Stuffed Roast Beef

No, Louisiana isn't an ingredient here. But the flavor of the great state sure is! Leftover alert! Lock some of this away in a vault for sandwiches on French bread the next day! Make two of your five guests go hungry, if necessary.

Makes 6 servings

1 onion

2 stalks celery

1 bell pepper

2 tablespoons unsalted butter

1 teaspoon salt

1 teaspoon white pepper

$3/4$ teaspoon black pepper

$3/4$ teaspoon minced garlic

$1/2$ teaspoon dry mustard

$1/2$ teaspoon ground cayenne

4 pounds boneless sirloin roast

1 Very finely, chop onions, celery, and bell pepper to make one cup of each.

2 In a bowl, mix together onions, celery, bell pepper, butter, salt, white pepper, black pepper, garlic, mustard, and cayenne.

QUICK ⬤ PAINLESS

Using a turkey baster or a narrow-spouted funnel will allow you to get all the ingredients of the vegetable mixture into the pockets of the roast. Another easy method is to put the mixture in a plastic baggie and cut off the corner or use a pastry bag so you can "pipe" it in.

3 Place roast in a large pan, fat side up. Using a large knife make 5 to 10 deep slits in the meat, forming pockets, down to a depth of about $1/2$ inch from the bottom; do not cut all the way through. Fill the pockets completely with the vegetable mixture, reserving a small amount of the vegetables to rub over the top of the roast.

4 Grill, covered, until a meat thermometer reads 160°F for medium doneness. For a rarer roast, only grill until thermometer reads 140°F. Serve immediately.

YOU'LL THANK YOURSELF LATER

Be sure to chop the vegetables in this recipe as finely as possible. It will allow you to use our method of getting them into the roast pockets more easily.

Remember! Be adventurous. Occasionally try something different. For example, on those days it's so hot outside you know you're going to want to drink all of the beer you have on hand, pour red wine over your Kooky Caraway Burgers instead.

Kooky Caraway Burgers

Caraway seeds, with their pleasant wintergreen-like scent, go well with many dishes. You'll find them to be fantastic on burgers as well.

Makes 6 servings

1 onion

1^1/2 pounds ground beef, chuck or round

1 teaspoon salt

1 teaspoon caraway seeds

1 teaspoon Worcestershire sauce

^{1}/4 teaspoon pepper

Optional: 1 cup beer, any American brand

1 Finely chop onion to make ^{1}/2 cup and, in a bowl, mix together with ground beef, salt, caraway seeds, Worcestershire Sauce, and pepper.

2 Shape mixture into 6 patties, each about 1-inch thick.

3 Place the patties in a shallow dish. Pour beer over the patties. Cover and refrigerate at 3 to 4 hours. (The patties may turn gray; this is okay.)

4 Remove patties from the marinade and grill 4 inches from heat, turning once, to the desired doneness, 15 to 20 minutes.

Florida Barbecued Spareribs

Florida, you say? Yep…there's cows in that thar state! And they know how to grow 'em, too. Who knows, maybe better than that state on the western side of the Gulf of Mexico. See what you think.

Makes 6 servings

2 cups butter

1 cup cider vinegar

1 cup catsup

One 6-ounce jar prepared horseradish

6 lemons, for juice

1 teaspoon salt

1 tablespoon Worcestershire sauce

1 teaspoon hot pepper sauce

5 pounds spareribs

1 In a medium-sized saucepan, melt butter over medium heat. Add vinegar, catsup, horseradish, the juice of the 6 lemons, salt, and Worcestershire and pepper sauces. Simmer uncovered 20 to 25 minutes to blend flavors. Use as basting sauce for spareribs.

2 Place ribs on grill 6 inches above hot coals. Brush with sauce and cook until brown on one side. Turn, brush once more with sauce, and brown the other side.

3 Turn and baste every 10 minutes until ribs are done, about 1 hour. Cut near bone in a center section of ribs and when juices run clear or golden, the ribs are done.

4 Place ribs on a platter and cut into 1 to 3 rib sections. Serve with any remaining sauce.

YOU'LL THANK YOURSELF LATER

Keep a spray bottle filled with water handy for this recipe. The butter in this sauce causes it to flame up when it hits the coals. If not, you might end up with "Charcoal Ribs" instead.

Gunny's Mediterranean Stuffed Steak

Quick and easy describes this steak. Oh, did we mention it tastes great? The black olives are the secret to this one. Mmmmm…

Makes 4 servings

1 clove garlic

$1/4$ cup sweet cream butter

$1/2$ teaspoon chives

$1/2$ teaspoon basil

Four 6- to 8-ounce sirloin steaks (at least 1 inch thick)

2 cups mushrooms

2 cups black olives

1 Mince garlic. Place butter, chives, basil, and garlic in microwave-safe container. Microwave for 15 seconds, or until butter is partially melted.

2 With very sharp knife (be careful, please, no finger-stuffed steaks here!), slit steaks along one edge, deeply enough to create a large, pita-like pocket.

3 Coat both sides of the pocket with butter and spice mixture.

4 Slice mushrooms and black olives thinly, and layer inside the steak; close pocket with a skewer.

5 Grill over medium-high heat, turning once, 10 to 12 minutes total.

Optional: Gunny tells us that before he places the steaks directly on the grill, he first "salt sears 'em" to enhance the flavor and seal in the juices. To add this step, put a cast-iron skillet over hot coals and once it's very hot, sprinkle $1/4$ teaspoon of salt in the skillet and one by one, slap in a steak. Flash sear each side of each steak for 15 to 30 seconds. Then grill according to the instructions in Step 5.

Getting Time on Your Side

	The Old Way	The Lazy Way
Convincing the family that your "merveilleux petit morceau de boeuf préparé de la interroger de façon serrée" special isn't incorrect French usage, nor is it a "hamburger"	30 minutes	0 minutes
Puckering up for a good steak	30 minutes	30 seconds (after the first bite, now that you know how to fix it)
Pondering which herbs to use to season your steaks	30 minutes	5 minutes
Time spent knowing each time you fired up the grill, you were probably going to star in another episode of one of those real disasters video shows	60 minutes	0 minutes
Contemplating how to serve leftover London broil	30 minutes	2 minutes
Trip to the emergency room for stitches due to that unfortunate knife-handling incident	360 minutes	0 minutes

nine

High-on-the-Hog Grill Fills

Everyone likes pork. Well, *almost* everyone. If you're a fan of our curly-tailed friend, please read on. Treats await you within the next few pages.

Pork isn't just the other white meat. Sure, we can choose between pork chops, pork steaks, pork tenderloin, pork roasts, or pork ribs. We'll leave the pork bellies to the commodities speculators, but even so, that still leaves us with pork sausage, bacon, and ham, too. How many tummies just growled? Raise your hands!

This chapter has more pork than the annual budget of the United States of America! But don't worry, you'll need no political maneuvering, or votes in Congress, to reap the rewards of these fantastic recipes.

So, with an oink, oink here, and an oink, oink there, let's break out the humble grillingware—we're off to hog heaven.

You can speed up the process if you allow your entrée to marinate outside of the refrigerator (as suggested in Step 3 of the Peachy Pork Steaks recipe). However, for safety's sake, don't let it set at room temperature for longer than 30 minutes.

Pleasing Peachy Pork Steaks

Here's one that'll even make our friends down in Georgia yell for more. Try this one out on the mother-in-law. You're sure to gain a few points with her after she tastes this dish.

Makes 4 servings

4 boneless pork chops/steaks (1-inch thick)
3 tablespoons lime or lemon juice
1 tablespoon vegetable oil
1 teaspoon ground cumin
Pinch cayenne pepper
Pinch black pepper

1 Arrange steaks side-by-side in shallow glass dish.

2 Stir together lime or lemon juice, oil, cumin, cayenne and black pepper.

3 Pour mixture over steaks; cover and marinate 30 minutes at room temperature or up to 4 hours in refrigerator. (If refrigerated, let steaks sit at room temperature for 30 minutes before grilling.)

4 Place steaks on grill over medium heat and reserve marinade.

5 Cook 6 to 8 minutes per side, brushing often with marinade. Do not overcook.

6 Serve with Peach Salad.

Peach Salad

Don't get stuck in the "it's pork so I've gotta serve it with applesauce" rut. Peaches please persnickety pork pundits, too. Try this recipe and see what we mean.

Makes 4 servings

2 ripe peaches

2 stalks green onion

Fresh cilantro

$1/2$ teaspoon red pepper flakes

$1/2$ teaspoon cumin

2 tablespoons lime or lemon juice

Salt and pepper to taste

1 Peel and dice peaches.

2 Chop onion finely to make 2 tablespoons and mince cilantro to make 1 tablespoon.

3 Mix together peaches, onion, cilantro, red pepper flakes, cumin, lime or lemon juice, salt, and pepper.

4 Allow to sit 30 minutes before serving beside pork chops or steaks.

QUICK ⬤ PAINLESS

Try using canned peaches for the Peach Salad. This will save you 5 to 10 minutes in preparation time. However, make sure you use peaches packed in natural juices, not syrup. The syrup is too sweet and will cover the taste of the spices in the recipe. You'll want your salad to pack its full punch!

Quick 'n' Easy Pork Roast

This is a great roast recipe which goes well with potato side dishes. If you're lucky, there'll be plenty remaining afterward, because the leftovers are better than the original!

Makes 4 servings

4 tablespoons brown mustard
3 pounds boneless pork roast
$1/4$ cup Tamari or soy sauce
$1/4$ teaspoon Tabasco pepper sauce

1 Apply mustard liberally on both sides of pork.

2 Mix Tamari or soy sauce and Tabasco pepper sauce.

3 Marinate roast in mixture 1 to 2 hours. (Turn once or twice.)

4 Place roast on hot grill and sear each side for 1 to 2 minutes.

5 Lower temperature and grill 20 minutes on each side or until done to your taste. Adjust time for larger or smaller roasts. The meat will taste best if not overcooked and still juicy.

Arizona Pork Tenderloin

Strap on your six-shooters to add to the feeling you're in the Old Southwest while eating these tenderloins. Just be careful where you point those things.

Makes 6 servings

5 garlic cloves

5 teaspoons chili powder

1^1/$_2$ teaspoons dried oregano

^{3}/$_4$ teaspoon ground cumin

1 tablespoon vegetable oil

5 pounds pork tenderloin

1 Crush garlic cloves.

2 In a small bowl, mix the chili powder, oregano, cumin, garlic, and vegetable oil.

3 Rub mixture over all surfaces of tenderloin.

4 Cover and refrigerate 2 to 24 hours.

5 Grill over medium heat for 15 to 20 minutes, turning occasionally. Slice and serve.

YOU'LL THANK YOURSELF LATER

If your tastebuds are more conservative, reduce the amount of chili powder used in this recipe to fit your individual preference.

You can save time by buying (Jamaican) jerk sauce in a bottle, as it is readily available in market condiment aisles. Simply marinate pork chops in sauce and cook as directed.

Spicy Jerk Pork Chops

Jerk seasoning is a Jamaican original which has spread in popularity, out of the Caribbean, to become a favorite pork and poultry seasoning of ours. Get ready, mon, these chops will have you listening to Bob Marley and the Wailers all night!

Makes 2 to 4 servings

$1/2$ cup yellow onion

Whole nutmeg

5 teaspoons dried thyme

5 teaspoons sugar

1 teaspoon salt

1 teaspoon ground allspice

1 teaspoon black pepper

$1/2$ teaspoon cayenne

$1/4$ teaspoon cinnamon

Four $1/2$-inch-thick rib pork chops (each about 4 ounces)

1 Mince the onion.

2 Grate $1/4$ teaspoon nutmeg.

3 Add thyme, sugar, salt, and allspice, black pepper, cayenne, and cinnamon and grind into a coarse paste.

4 Pat pork chops dry and rub both sides with the jerk paste.

5 Oil grill rack with vegetable oil.

6 Grill 4 minutes on each side, or until cooked through.

Orange-Glazed Baby Back Ribs

What is it that makes oranges and pork go well together? We don't know, but we're glad they do because they are a match made in heaven!

Makes 4 to 8 servings

$^2/_3$ cup honey

$^1/_2$ cup fresh orange juice

2 tablespoons Worcestershire sauce

2 tablespoons minced orange peel (orange part only)

1 tablespoon minced garlic

1 tablespoon soy sauce

4 to 5 pounds baby back pork ribs

1. In large container, mix together honey, orange juice, Worcestershire sauce, orange peel, garlic, and soy sauce.

2. Fork-pierce meaty areas of ribs and place in container with marinade. Cover and refrigerate for 6 to 24 hours.

3. Grill over medium to high heat until cooked through, turning occasionally. Grilling time will be approximately 25 minutes, depending on the heat of the grill, cut of the ribs, and distance from coals.

YOU'LL THANK YOURSELF LATER

Once you remove meat from the marinade, pour the marinade into a cast-iron skillet and set it where it can simmer on the back of your grill. It'll be close by when you need it for basting and you'll be "decontaminating" it in the process.

Florida Sunshine Pork Steaks

Here's a great recipe that tends to drive everyone within smelling distance crazy while it's cooking. You'll be so anxious to taste this one, you'll want to take it off the grill before it's time, but trust us, you'll be glad you waited.

Makes 4 to 6 servings

2 pounds pork steaks, $3/4$ inch thick

Marinade

$1/2$ cup orange juice, fresh or packaged

3 tablespoons brown sugar

3 tablespoons cider vinegar

$1/4$ teaspoon salt

$1/2$ teaspoon dry mustard

$1/4$ teaspoon ground ginger

2 tablespoons catsup

1 In a shallow glass dish, mix all marinade ingredients. Add pork steaks. Cover dish with plastic wrap or foil. Refrigerate 6 to 24 hours.

2 Allow steaks to sit at room temperature for 30 minutes before grilling.

3 Place steaks on grill over medium heat and reserve marinade.

4 Grill 4 to 6 minutes per side, basting the steaks often with the marinade.

Tangy Citrus Pork Chops

Baked potatoes topped with butter and a couple pinches of rosemary make these chops irresistible. For an extra added treat, sprinkle garlic and a few drops of Worcestershire sauce on bread and toast on the grill. It's great!

Makes 3 to 6 servings

Bunch of fresh parsley

2 cloves garlic

2 tablespoons olive oil

1 tablespoon fresh rosemary, chopped

1 tablespoon grated orange peel

1 tablespoon grated lemon peel

1 teaspoon sugar

$1/2$ teaspoon dry oregano

$1/2$ teaspoon salt

$1/2$ teaspoon black pepper

Six $1/2$-inch-thick pork chops

1 Chop parsley and mince garlic.

2 In a bowl, mix together parsley, garlic, oil, rosemary, orange and lemon peel, sugar, oregano, salt, and pepper.

3 Spread mixture over each chop. Cover and refrigerate overnight.

4 Scrape away as much of the marinade as possible and grill for 2 to 3 minutes on each side.

QUICK 🐷 PAINLESS

While you preheat the grill, thaw some pork chops or steaks. For each 4 chops, sauté 1 minced clove garlic in 1 table-spoon of olive oil, or do a quickie fake sauté by putting the garlic and oil in the microwave on high for 20 seconds. Rub the oil on both sides of each chop and grill several minutes on each side, depending on the thickness of the chops. No other seasoning is needed. Serve with a salad.

Garlic and Honey Pork Chops

Keith first tried this one on Labor Day a couple of years back and it was perfect. However, as you'll see, it fits well anytime of the year. Try it out with stir-fried vegetables and you get the chance to improve on perfection.

Makes 4 servings

2 cloves garlic
2 tablespoons soy sauce
$^1/_4$ cup honey
$^1/_4$ cup lemon juice
1 tablespoon cooking sherry
Four 1- to 1$^1/_2$-inch boneless pork chops

1 Chop and mince garlic.

2 In a 1-cup measuring cup, mix garlic, soy sauce, honey, lemon juice, and sherry well.

3 Pour mixture over chops in a shallow glass dish. Cover and refrigerate overnight.

4 Secure aluminum foil on grill 15 minutes before cooking.

5 Remove chops from dish, allowing marinade to drip away.

6 Reserve leftover marinade.

QUICK ⬤ PAINLESS

Pour your liquid ingredients (the honey and lemon juice in the Garlic and Honey Pork Chop recipe) into a glass measuring cup first; then add the other ingredients that either require you use a measuring spoon (soy sauce, sherry) or whose amounts can vary slightly (garlic cloves). You get an accurate amount and you'll save yourself from dirtying a mixing bowl in the process—you can stir it all up in the cup.

7 Place chops on foil. Raise grill to medium height or reduce heat to medium if using gas grill.

8 Cook for 16 to 18 minutes, turning occasionally, until done.

9 Boil reserve marinade for 3 to 4 minutes. Serve over chops.

YOU'LL THANK YOURSELF LATER

Be careful when using a grill fork that you don't pierce the meat so deeply that all of the good juices "leak" out.

Deep South Pork Roast

The weather isn't the only thing they like hot in the South. And, as you'll discover in this recipe, they don't just add a touch of "shugah" to their voices. Y'all will like the sweet 'n' tangy mergin' in this dish, darlin'.

Makes 10 to 20 servings

3 cloves garlic

1 teaspoon parsley

1 large onion

2 tablespoons steak sauce (Lea & Perrins)

1 to 2 teaspoons seasoned salt (dry rub)

$1/2$ cup Tiger Sauce (brand name sweetened hot sauce)

$1/2$ cup Worcestershire sauce

$2^1/2$ tablespoons dry mustard

10 pounds boneless pork roast

One 6-ounce can of tomato paste

3 tablespoons brown sugar

1 Chop garlic, parsley, and onion.

2 In a small bowl, mix together the garlic, parsley, steak sauce, onion, Tiger Sauce, Worcestershire sauce, and dry mustard.

3 Use the seasoned salt to rub the entire outside of the roast, pressing the salt into the meat as you go.

4 Make several deep slits into the roast, being careful not to puncture the opposite side. Fill slits with sauce and rub over the outside of the roast well.

IF YOU'RE SO INCLINED

You can employ some of the optional grilling equipment we covered in Chapter 2 to help make a good Deep South Pork Roast great if you:

■ Use a basting syringe to place sauce into the slits in the roast.

■ Have a meat thermometer handy while cooking the roast. Since meat sizes differ, exact cooking times for roasts are difficult to determine.

5 Place roast in container, cover, and refrigerate for 6 hours or overnight.

6 In another small bowl, mix tomato paste and brown sugar well. Set aside.

7 Grill roast with lid closed, until the internal temperature reaches 170°F.

8 Brush with tomato paste and brown sugar mixture when done.

QUICK ⬤⬤ PAINLESS

For those times you need crushed garlic and don't have a base or a garlic press handy, you can place the peeled garlic cloves between pieces of waxed paper and whack 'em a few times with a hammer.

Keith's Pensacola Porkribs

These are great ribs! Tender and tasty, they are good any time of year. The best part is the Dr. Pepper—it tenderizes the meat and provides a different flavor from the usual rib recipes. This one is a "must taste"!

Makes 8 to 12 servings

$1^1/_2$ cups catsup

$^3/_4$ cup brown sugar

$^3/_8$ cup honey

4 tablespoons soy sauce

One 12-ounce can of Dr. Pepper

4 to 6 pounds baby back pork ribs

Pepper to taste

1   Mix together catsup, brown sugar, honey, soy sauce, and Dr. Pepper in a large container.

2   Fork-pierce meaty areas of ribs and place in container with marinade. Cover and refrigerate for 6 to 24 hours.

3   Place ribs on grill over a medium to high heat, and lightly add pepper to taste.

4   Grill until cooked through, turning occasionally, 25 minutes total.

Sometimes it's best not to question why something works—just accept that it does. The good folks at Dr. Pepper may know exactly why their drink tenderizes meat, but we don't. Sit back and soak up the compliments you'll get from family and friends when they try these tender flavorful ribs! (Pam is still trying to create a Mountain Dew recipe.)

The Lazy Way

Getting Time on Your Side

	The Old Way	The Lazy Way
Slaving over a hot stove, frying pork chops	30 minutes	0 minutes
Pondering what you can serve with your pork dish since you're out of applesauce	15 minutes	1 minute (the time it takes to turn to the Peach Salad recipe in this chapter)
Crushing garlic	5 minutes (chopping it really fine)	2 minutes (using the waxed paper-hammer method)
Crushing garlic	5 minutes (chopping it really fine)	30 seconds (measuring out 1/4 teaspoon of Minor's Signature™ garlic concentrate)
Slow-marinating a pork roast	4 to 48 hours (marinating the roast in the refrigerator)	30 minutes (marinating the roast at room temperature), 5 minutes (using a basting syringe)
Washing your mixing bowl	3 minutes	0 minutes (when you mix up your marinade in the measuring cup

Seafood – And They Will, And They Will, Sizzle Right on the Grill

It's time now for some recipes for which you'll fall hook, line, and sinker. They're all keepers. You won't be tempted to throw a single one back.

Those familiar with P. G. Wodehouse's novels know that character Bertie Wooster is convinced that his butler Jeeves is so smart because of all of the fish he eats.

Whether or not seafood is *brain food* is open to speculation. What is known is that fish does have definite benefits. Not only is it our leanest source of protein, it's heart healthy in other ways, too.

The omega-3 essential fatty acids found in fish help lower triglyceride (bad blood fat) levels, which increase the risk of coronary artery disease. Because they alter the ability of platelets to stick together, omega-3 fatty acids also act as a natural anticoagulant which reduces the chances of dangerous

Keep in mind you can always adjust recipes to your own tastes or to accommodate the ingredients you have on hand. For example, at times we've used ground ginger and candied ginger instead of the grated fresh ginger used in this recipe.

blood clotting. And, as if that isn't enough, studies show they also appear to lower blood pressure as well.

So, now that you're home from the seafood market, take off those waders and get ready to jump right in!

It's Gingery Grilled Grouper Steak Lime

Ginger may have left the Spice Girls, but ginger will never leave our spice racks. Once you taste this recipe, you'll know why.

Makes 6 servings

Fresh ginger root
$^1/_4$ cup fresh lime juice (2 to 3 limes)
2 tablespoons olive oil
1 clove garlic
1 tablespoon soy sauce
1 teaspoon Dijon-style mustard
$^1/_4$ teaspoon salt
$^1/_4$ teaspoon freshly ground black pepper
6 grouper steaks (about 1-inch thick)

1 Grate ginger root to make 1 teaspoon.

2 In a small bowl, mix together the lime juice, olive oil, finely chopped garlic, soy sauce, ginger, Dijon mustard, and salt and pepper.

3 Divide the marinade into two portions, using half to brush the grouper. Reserve the remaining marinade in a separate small bowl.

4 Place fish on a medium grill, and cook until the steaks are golden on the outside and done to taste inside, 5 to 7 minutes per side.

5 Remove the fish steaks from the grill and place them on a serving platter or onto individual plates. Drizzle some of the reserved lime mixture over each steak.

QUICK ⬛ PAINLESS

Gingery Grilled Grouper Steak Lime works with any type of firm fish steak. Just keep in mind that if your steaks are thinner than 1 inch, you'll need to reduce the cooking time slightly. Of course, if they are thicker, you'll want to increase the cooking time accordingly.

IF YOU'RE SO
INCLINED

If you're growing fennel in this year's herb garden, omit the seed from the Fine Fenneled Swordfish recipe and snip some fresh fennel leaves over the fish instead. Or use the feathery fresh fennel leaves as a garnish instead of parsley.

A Fine Fenneled Swordfish

The fennel seeds give this recipe a distinctive flavor. For a change of pace, you can substitute butter for the olive oil; just keep in mind that if you do, you'll need to watch it a bit more closely as it grills so the steaks don't burn.

Makes 4 servings

Fresh parsley
3 tablespoons fresh lemon juice
4 tablespoons olive oil
2 tablespoons fennel seeds
$1/2$ teaspoon salt
2 garlic cloves
4 swordfish steaks ($1/2$ pound each)

1 Chop parsley finely to make 2 tablespoons.

2 In a small bowl, mix the lemon juice, olive oil, fennel seeds, salt, finely chopped garlic, and parsley. Pour over the fish and marinate it in the refrigerator, covered, for 4 to 6 hours.

3 Grill the steaks over white-hot coals for 5 minutes on each side.

Favorite Garlic Grilled Shrimp

Keith sometimes likes to omit the water chestnuts and serve the shrimp in this recipe on crusty bakery rolls as gourmet po-boys (Louisiana's version of the sandwich known as a hero to some of us, a submarine to others).

Makes 12 servings

$1/2$ cup butter

2 teaspoons garlic salt

$1/8$ teaspoon red pepper sauce

One 8-oz. can sliced water chestnuts

1 large green pepper

1 slice onion

$1/2$ teaspoon salt

$1/2$ teaspoon dried tarragon leaves

3 pounds cleaned raw shrimp

1   Form a pan, 11 x 11 x $1/2$ inch, from double thickness heavy duty aluminum foil. Place butter, garlic salt, and red pepper sauce in pan.

2   Chop onion slice to equal 1 tablespoon.

3   Place pan on grill 4 to 6 inches from medium coals until butter is melted. Remove pan from grill and add the drained water chestnuts, green pepper rings, chopped onion, salt, and tarragon. Mix well, being careful not to tear the foil pan. Clean the shrimp and add it to the pan, tossing them with the seasoning mixture.

4   Cover the pan with a piece of heavy duty aluminum foil, sealing edges well. Grill until shrimp are done, 20 to 30 minutes.

QUICK 🔲 PAINLESS

Feel free to use a disposable foil pan instead of making one out of foil; then you only need to create the lid.

Love That Lemon Shrimp

Seafood is a bit more economical in Keith's neck o' the woods, so he sometimes serves these on sandwiches, too. Pam, on the other hand, is from the Midwest, where the motto seems to be: "We'll let you buy seafood, but we're gonna make you pay big time if you do." Therefore, she likes to present the shrimp directly on each serving plate, so she and her guests can get a good look at (read: appreciate) each and every one of them!

Makes 4 servings

2 pounds large shrimp

Parsley

3 cloves garlic

1 medium-sized onion

1 teaspoon dry mustard

1 teaspoon salt

$1/2$ cup olive oil

3 tablespoons fresh lemon juice

1 Rinse the shrimp, then snip the shells down the back, being careful that the shells remain on. Place the shrimp in a bowl large enough to hold them and the marinade.

2 Chop parsley finely to make $1/2$ cup. Chop garlic and onion finely.

3 In a small bowl, combine the finely chopped garlic and onion, dry mustard, salt, olive oil, lemon juice, and parsley. Pour the mixture over the shrimp.

4 Cover and marinate the shrimp in the refrigerator for 10 to 30 minutes. (If you plan to use bamboo skewers to grill the shrimp, now is the time to soak them in water so they'll be ready when the shrimp is.)

5 Place the shrimp on a grill rack over hot coals. Cook the shrimp for 5 to 8 minutes, turning them once. Serve them in their shells.

YOU'LL THANK YOURSELF LATER

Keep moustache scissors cleaned and ready in your kitchen. They come in handy for snipping the shells, as called for in Love That Lemon Shrimp.

Do you brown bag your lunch? Leftover grilled shrimp is delicious in a tossed salad. Add the dressing when you're ready to eat and you have a complete meal!

We'll Have a Hot Time on the Ol' Shrimp Tonight!

Man doesn't live by mild alone. Sometimes he just feels the need for something to add some sizzle in his life. Here's a painless, palate-pleasing way to do just that.

Makes 6 servings

Parsley

4 tablespoons olive oil

1 teaspoon salt

$1/2$ teaspoon pepper

$1/2$ teaspoon garlic powder

6 tablespoons chili sauce

6 tablespoons vinegar

2 tablespoons Worcestershire sauce

$1/8$ teaspoon liquid hot pepper sauce

2 tablespoons melted butter

2 pounds large shrimp

1 Chop parsley finely to make $1/2$ cup.

2 In a small bowl, mix the olive oil, salt, pepper, garlic powder, chili sauce, vinegar, Worcestershire sauce, hot pepper sauce, parsley, and melted butter. Pour over shelled and deveined shrimp; cover and refrigerate for up to 1 hour.

3 Remove shrimp from marinade. (You can reserve the left-over portion of the mixture to serve alongside the shrimp if you remember to first boil it to destroy any bacteria introduced by the raw shrimp.) Either thread shrimp onto skewers or put them on a pan made of two pieces of greased heavy-duty aluminum foil. If using skewers, be sure to grease the grill rack or spray it with non-stick cooking spray. Grill the shrimp about 4 to 6 inches above a bed of low-glowing coals.

4 Cook for 4 minutes on each side or until shrimp turn pink, turning them at least once. Baste with the reserved (boiled) marinade, if you wish.

YOU'LL THANK YOURSELF LATER

You can save money if you also cut up some grilled hot dog wheels and serve them on a children's plate alongside the shrimp. Dip for that appetizer is easy too—catsup!

Grilled Whole Lobster

Lobster is so sweet and delicious, it needs little embellishment. We like to add some lemon juice to the butter. That choice is yours, as is adding the salt, pepper, or tarragon—or other seasonings, for that matter. The nice thing about eating this dish outside is that you can forget the lobster bib. Just hose yourself down when you're done eating!

Per lobster

$1/2$ cup butter

$1/4$ cup lemon juice

1 whole lobster

Optional: Salt

Pepper

$1/8$ teaspoon dried whole tarragon

1. In a small bowl, melt the butter in the microwave, then add the lemon juice. (If you insist, you can add salt, pepper, and the tarragon to the mixture now, too.)

2. Place each lobster on its back (belly up) and split it from head to tail. Remove all internal tracks including the sac. Create a foil packet large enough to generously hold the lobster (shell side down) out of two sheets of heavy-duty aluminum foil. Bring the foil up and over the lobster, crimping and folding it on the sides to create a container. Pour the melted butter and lemon juice mixture in through the top opening, crimp and seal one layer of foil, then do the same with the next layer to create a double seal.

QUICK ⬤ PAINLESS

Prefer steamed lobster? Then substitute water for the butter and lemon juice. Grill according to the instructions for Grilled Whole Lobster. Serve with melted butter and a lemon wedge.

3 Place packet on grill so shell side is facing down. Grill over a medium heat for 5 minutes. Turn the packet and cook for another 6 to 8 minutes.

How best to eat a lobster can seem intimidating at first. However, it's easy! Just follow these steps:

1. Twist off the large claws and crack open. (Some like to suck the meat out of the claws.)

2. Break off the tail and remove the flippers. Using a lobster fork, push the tail meat out in one piece. (Remove and disgard the black vein.)

3. Crack open the body.

4. Break off each of the small walking legs attached to the body.

YOU'LL THANK YOURSELF LATER

Make sure you eat every succulent morsel of your lobster. You'll want to suck the meat out of the small walking legs, too.

Grilled Snapper Fillets with Lime-Orange Marinade

Great! There's that tarragon again! No, we're not in some sort of wicked herbalist-induced tarragon trance. Tarragon complements seafood; therefore, it is our friend!

Makes 4 servings

Bunch shallots or scallions

$^1/_4$ cup lime juice

$^1/_4$ cup orange juice

1 tablespoon olive oil

2 tablespoons fresh tarragon

$^1/_8$ teaspoon ground nutmeg

$1^1/_4$ pounds red snapper fillets

1 lime

1 orange

1 Mince shallot or scallions to make 2 tablespoons.

2 In a shallow bowl large enough to hold the fillets and marinade, combine lime juice, orange juice, oil, shallots or scallions, tarragon and nutmeg. Place red snapper fillets in bowl, turning to coat evenly with marinade. Marinate, skin side up, covered, in the refrigerator for 1 hour.

IF YOU'RE SO INCLINED

While tarragon is delicious in many seafood recipes, this essential "fine herbes" member (chives, chervil, and parsley being the others) adds a savory difference when added to sour cream or French dressing, melted butter sauce, mayonnaise, and tartar sauce.

3 Cook fillets on a hot grill, skin side up, for 3 minutes. Turn fillets over, baste with marinade and grill for another 3 to 6 minutes.

4 Slice lime and orange into $1/2$-inch slices. Place on grill and baste lightly with marinade. Turn once and serve the fruit with the fish fillets.

It's easy to make changes to the Grilled Oysters au Gratin recipe. Simply use a different type of cracker.

Grilled Oysters au Gratin

Pam bakes an escalloped oyster dish every Christmas. Sometimes the oyster craving hits during the summer, so she prepares them this way instead. For those times she's in a hurry, she beats an egg into the reserved oyster liquid, mixes all of the remaining ingredients together, and puts them in a foil-covered aluminum pan to bake over indirect heat for about 45 minutes while she grills the rest of the meal.

Makes 6 to 8 servings

2 cups fine cracker crumbs

1 teaspoon salt

1 quart shucked oysters

$^1/_2$ pound butter, melted

1 In a shallow dish, mix the cracker crumbs with the salt. Roll the oysters well in a clean napkin to make them as dry as possible. Thrust a fork through the tough muscle of each oyster.

2 Next, dip each oyster into the crumbs, then into the butter, then into the crumbs again.

3 Arrange the oysters in a hinged wire grill and broil them over hot coals for 3 minutes, turning the wire grill every 5 or 10 seconds to prevent the cracker coating from burning.

4 When the oysters are plump and the juices run clear, they are done. Serve immediately.

Shellfish Grill

Neat! Now you can enjoy your own seafood smorgasbord!

Makes 4 servings

40 clams

20 medium-sized oysters

$^1/_4$ cup butter or margarine

1 Scrub the clams and oysters. Place butter in a grill-safe pan on outer edge of grill to melt and keep warm.

2 Set clams and oysters on the grill 4 to 6 inches above a solid bed of glowing coals. After 4 minutes or when clams and oysters begin to open, turn them over and continue to cook until they pop wide open, 3 to 4 minutes.

3 Hold clams and oysters over butter pan to drain juices into butter. Pluck out meat with a fork, dip in butter and eat.

YOU'LL THANK YOURSELF LATER

Always be sure to clean the shellfish well when you're cooking them in the shell. This will assure that no sand, sediment, or other untasty morsels get onto your plate later.

Follow the recipes in this chapter and you'll be doing double duty in one easy step—serving heart healthy *and* delicious meals.

Grilled Tuna Steaks

12 servings? Not to worry! If you don't need to serve an army, simply divide the recipe accordingly. Just plan on getting your tuna fork ready to set the pitch for anyone who's fortunate enough to get to eat this dish.

Makes 12 servings

Twelve 1-inch-thick tuna steaks

1 cup lemon juice

1/2 cup soy sauce

2 bay leaves

1/2 teaspoon dried whole thyme

1 Place steaks in a large shallow container. Combine lemon juice, soy sauce, bay leaves, and thyme in a small bowl, stir well, then pour the mixture over fish. Cover and refrigerate 1 hour, turning fish frequently.

2 Remove fish from marinade. Place remaining marinade in a grill-safe pan at the back of the grill to bring it to a boil to destroy any bacteria introduced by the fish.

3 Place tuna steaks in greased wire grilling baskets. Grill over hot coals 20 minutes or until fish flakes easily with a fork. Turn and baste occasionally with marinade.

Easy as ABC: Add Balsamic Cod

We recommend you mix up an extra batch of this marinade using extra virgin olive oil, divide it in half, and call the extra "vinaigrette." It's delicious drizzled over the greens and veggies in your sidedish salad. (This marinade is delicious with shrimp and scallops, too.)

Makes 4 servings

$1/4$ cup olive oil

$1/8$ cup balsamic vinegar

1 shallot

$1^1/2$ teaspoon Dijon mustard

$1/2$ teaspoon thyme or fennel seeds

1 tablespoon white wine vinegar

4 cod fillets, about $1/2$ pound each

1 In a glass dish large enough to hold cod fillets, mix together the olive oil, balsamic vinegar, finely chopped shallot, Dijon mustard, thyme or fennel seeds (according to your taste preference), and the white wine vinegar.

2 Add the cod fillets and allow to marinate for 30 minutes at room temperature, or cover the dish with plastic wrap and marinate in the refrigerator overnight.

3 Grill on an oiled rack over hot coals for 4 to 5 minutes per side.

IF YOU'RE SO INCLINED

Pour a batch of the Easy as ABC: Add Balsamic Cod marinade (a.k.a. vinaigrette) over a can of drained artichoke hearts. Whether you let the artichokes "marinate" overnight in a covered glass dish or immediately toss 'em with your salad greens and veggies, you'll love the results!

Aloha-Sesame Albacore

Get out that grass skirt and get ready to wiggle your way to a mighty fine meal. Just be careful not to overcook it; albacore tends to dry out quickly. This sauce is great on other firm white fish or chicken breasts, too.

Makes 4 servings

Fresh ginger root

$^1/_3$ cup soy sauce

$^1/_4$ cup dry white wine

4 tablespoons butter

2 tablespoons sugar

1 clove garlic, crushed

4 albacore steaks, each about $^1/_2$ pound

8 slices bacon

8 tablespoons butter

6 tablespoons lemon juice

$^1/_4$ cup dry sherry

$^1/_4$ cup sesame seeds

lemon wedges

1 Grate ginger to make $^3/_4$ tablespoon.

2 In a small bowl, combine the soy sauce, dry white wine, melted butter, sugar, ginger, and garlic and mix well to make a marinade. Place the albacore steaks in a shallow dish, pour in $^1/_2$ cup of the marinade, cover, and refrigerate for one hour.

3 Remove steaks from marinade and wrap each piece of fish with two bacon slices, and fasten the bacon with wooden picks (that you've soaked in water).

4 In a small grill-safe pan, melt the 8 tablespoons of butter and remove from heat. Stir in the remaining marinade, the lemon juice, and sherry.

5 Arrange the tuna on an oiled grill rack over medium-hot coals, then brush with a generous amount of the butter mixture.

6 When the steaks are done on one side (after 8 to 10 minutes), sprinkle them with sesame seeds, turn them over, and cook them until the other side is brown. Baste the fish again with the butter mixture and sprinkle them with the remaining sesame seeds.

7 Before serving, turn the steaks over once more to toast all the seeds. Total cooking time should be 15 minutes. Serve with a lemon wedge on each plate.

Seafood dishes are often so rich and wonderful that it's enough to limit your menu to a main seafood course and a simple salad. We often place a crusty loaf of French bread in a basket or on a cutting board with a knife so it's there for those who want it; you can also put some butter pats floating in a bowl of ice chips if you wish. (Pluck a flower blossom from your garden to place in the middle of that bowl for an impressive touch.) We've given you the map; it's up to you as to which route you take to make the journey. Happy travels!

QUICK ⬤ PAINLESS

Grow your own garnish! Check the local nursery for one of the wonderful dwarf varieties of curly parsley. They grow well in containers and require little fuss. The rich green leaves look great next to the delicate white flesh of you fish entrée.

Getting Time on Your Side

	The Old Way	The Lazy Way
Clogging your arteries	30 minutes	0 minutes
Avoiding cod because you think it'll make you have cod liver oil flashbacks	30 minutes	0 minutes
Fishing for compliments	30 minutes	0 minutes (They happen automatically when you prepare the recipes in this chapter!)
Wondering what made Jeeves so smart	5 minutes (a day)	0 minutes (because you read the chapter intro)
Time spent getting the "fish smell" out of the house	60 minutes (after you finish cleaning up the "frying" splatters)	0 minutes
Pondering fine fenneled flavor	30 minutes	30 minutes (except now you're savoring it, too)

Meats That Prove Variety Is the Nice of Life

If it looks like a duck, walks like a duck, and quacks like a duck…it's not dressed and ready for the grill.

Otherwise, assuming that your main course can't still get up and walk away, our goal in this chapter is to give you suggestions on how to prepare it.

As you read the recipes in this chapter, we remind you that the serving suggestions are just that—suggestions. Some appetites are…hmmm, shall we say healthier?…than others. Plus, the amount of meat after grilling time can vary dramatically. A 5 pound free-range duck can probably be quartered for four servings; a wild duck of the same size—if you can find one that large—oftentimes will barely serve two. When in doubt, ask your butcher. Unless you're on a diet, just remember to look in his eyes so you can concentrate on what he says; avoid glances at his apron.

All It's Quacked Up to Be Roast Duck

Choose your red wine for this recipe according to your tastes. Burgundy or port are fine, or use a sweet fruity wine if you like. Some grill chefs like to flambé the duck as their final step in preparing this dish.

Makes 2 servings

One 5-pound duck
Salt
Pepper
1 small orange
Duck liver
$^1/_2$ cup butter
$^1/_2$ cup red wine

1 Wash the duck, pat dry, prick the skin with a fork and rub with salt and pepper to taste. Cut the orange in half, and place it and the duck liver inside the cavity. (Some cooks truss the bird at this point. Your call.)

2 In a small saucepan (you'll eventually remove from the heat and keep close by on your grill shelf so you can baste this dish frequently throughout the "roasting" process), melt the butter and stir in red wine.

3 Brush the duck with the butter wine mixture and place it breast side up in a hot grill, close the grill lid, and grill for 15 minutes.

QUICK ☜☞ PAINLESS

For a successful flambé, preheat the liqueur. That way, it'll ignite instantly when you touch the flame to it. Also, choose a liqueur that complements the dish, such as Triple Sec for à l'orange dishes.

4 Reduce your grill setting to low. Continue grilling the duck, allowing 20 minutes per pound, basting frequently with the butter and wine sauce.

5 Remove from the grill, place on a platter and let rest for 10 minutes. To serve, cut the duck into two halves.

To keep the meat moist and the skin crispy, place a pan of water inside your closed grill while you roast the duck. If you can move the coals, place them around a drip pan filled with water. Using the indirect method on your gas grill, set a pan of water over the warmer portion of the grill.

This sauce is a perfect answer if you have a tougher cut of beef to marinate. The vinegar acts as a tenderizing agent.

The Swiss Army Knife Equivalent of Barbecue Sauces

Some people swear that this sauce stores well at room temperature. We prefer to keep it in the refrigerator in quart jars. The catsup imparts a subtle tomato flavor. The vinegar will tenderize about any meat, which makes this sauce perfect for wild game. In fact, we've simmered "gamey" cuts overnight, covering them with water to which we've added $1/3$ to 1 cup of cider vinegar. The next morning, we pour off that water and replace it with the Swiss Army Knife Sauce.

Makes 12 cups (or 3 quarts)

$1/2$ cup brown sugar

$1/2$ cup Worcestershire sauce

$1/2$ cup Dijon mustard

$1 1/3$ cup catsup

$1/8$ cup black pepper

1 tablespoon red pepper flakes

1 quart (4 cups) red wine vinegar

$2 2/3$ cups water

$1 1/3$ cups white wine

$1/2$ cup salt

This recipe is best made in advance on your stovetop.

1 Pour all ingredients into a large stainless steel pot and bring to a boil. Reduce the heat and simmer for 30 minutes, covered. Allow to cool and measure into quart jars to store in the refrigerator.

Mousse and Squirrel

Okay, indulge us. We'll admit we included this one just so we could use the recipe name. You'll find the recipe for Who Goosed the Mousse? in Chapter 15 on desserts. Otherwise, this is just one more example of how you can use The Swiss Army Knife Equivalent of Barbecue Sauces.

Makes 2 servings

- 1 squirrel
- 1 cup of the Swiss Army Knife Equivalent of Barbecue Sauces

1. Split or cut the squirrel into two halves lengthwise and place cut side down in a rectangle glass baking dish.

2. Pour the cup of sauce over the squirrel. Cover the dish with plastic wrap and refrigerate from 1 to 24 hours.

3. Grill over medium coals for 20 to 25 minutes, turning once.

IF YOU'RE SO
INCLINED

Wild game does often have a richer flavor, so you may want to counter that taste with subtler side dishes. Fruit dishes are always a good choice: all-natural blueberry preserves on crusty bread, for example. Or raspberry vinaigrette dressing on a spinach salad. Or a baked potato and fresh fruit or a sorbet for dessert. Is your mouth watering yet?

Once you have the
bratwurst simmering
in the beer, take a
break. Go ahead and
indulge! Have a beer or
a lemonade. You've got
the time now.

The Lazy Way

Bratwurst and Beer

*Presto! Chango! To turn these from good sandwiches to great
ones, spread stone ground mustard on some deli buns and
toast them on the grill.*

Makes 4 servings

4 bratwurst

1 bag sauerkraut

One 12-ounce can of beer

1 tablespoon dried minced onion

1 Place bratwurst on the rack over medium hot coals and
grill them while you prepare the sauerkraut, turning them
often to keep them from burning. This step allows the
bratwurst to absorb some delicious smoke flavor created
when the fat drips off of them—plus there's the added
bonus of reducing some of the fat content.

2 If you want to remove some of the "kick" from the sauerkraut, first place it in a colander and rinse well. Put a
heavy iron skillet on the grill and add the sauerkraut, can
of beer, and minced onion. Bring to a boil and then move
skillet to a cooler portion of the grill. Add the bratwurst to
the skillet, cover, and allow to simmer for 30 minutes to an
hour. Put a bratwurst and a generous amount of sauerkraut on a toasted bun and enjoy.

Saucy Horseradish Leg of Lamb

Just 'cause it's lamb doesn't mean it has to be served with mint. And horseradish isn't just for roast beef (although this seasoning is great on a beef roast as well). Dare to be different!

Makes 6 to 8 servings

$^1/_2$ cup prepared horseradish

$^1/_2$ teaspoon ground black pepper

1 teaspoon finely shredded lemon peel

4 teaspoons lemon juice

$^1/_2$ cup butter, melted

One 6-pound leg of lamb

1 In a small mixing bowl, combine horseradish, pepper, lemon peel, and lemon juice. Stir melted butter into horseradish mixture. Spoon desired portion of rub into a small bowl and brush it onto meat before grilling. This recipe makes about 1 cup or enough for 4 to 6 pounds meat. (Leftovers can be stored up to 2 weeks in the refrigerator. Reheat to melt butter before using.)

2 Rub the horseradish sauce into the meat. Use the indirect method to grill the leg of lamb for $1^1/_2$ hours or until the temperature on the meat thermometer reaches 160°F for medium. Brush with additional Saucy Horseradish several times during the grilling process.

IF YOU'RE SO
INCLINED

For those times you're in a hurry, season butterflied lamb chops with Saucy Horseradish rub and grill those instead of a leg of lamb.

Gobble 'Em Turkey Burgers

These go well with your standard condiments. Or try providing some chutney or salsa instead. Put 'em on buns or alongside a salad. They'll disappear quickly, no matter how you serve 'em.

Makes 8 servings

1 Vidalia onion

1 yellow or red bell pepper

1 cup fresh mushrooms, chopped

2 teaspoons garlic, finely minced

1 teaspoon olive oil

1 tomato

1 carrot

2 pounds ground turkey

1 egg

$^1/_2$ cup fresh bread crumbs

1 tablespoon Maggi seasoning

Salt

Freshly ground pepper to taste

1 Chop onion, then seed and chop pepper. Chop mushrooms and mince garlic.

2 Place a grill-safe sauté pan on the rack and heat the pan. Pour 1 teaspoon of olive oil into the pan, and when it begins to sizzle, sauté onions, transferring them to a large bowl to cool slightly while you sauté the pepper. Transfer the pepper to the bowl and sauté the mushrooms, then the garlic. Add scant amounts of additional olive oil as needed.

A COMPLETE WASTE OF TIME

The 3 Worst Things You Can Do with Turkey:

1. Buy a turkey that's too large for your grill (you'll need to be able to close the grill lid).

2. Forget to allow sufficient time for frozen turkey to thaw.

3. Only serve turkey on Thanksgiving.

3 Seed, peel, and chop tomato. Peel and finely grate carrots. Sauté.

4 Add the ground turkey, egg, bread crumbs, and Maggi seasoning to the vegetables. Mix well.

5 Form mixture into 8 burger patties. Lightly spray patties with olive oil spray and place on grill. Grill burgers for 5 to 6 minutes on each side, until they are browned and firm to the touch.

6 Season with salt and pepper to taste. Serve immediately.

YOU'LL THANK YOURSELF LATER

Don't panic if you don't have any Maggi seasoning on hand—although you may want to go ahead and order some from Allserv (http://allserv.com/quikorde.htm). For this batch, substitute 1 tablespoon of soy sauce and, if you're daring, an experimental dash of another seasoning such as basil or horseradish.

LET'S TALK TURKEY

We're about to share three different methods for grilling a turkey. Regardless of the one you use, please be safe and DO NOT STUFF your turkey with dressing. You can still fix your dressing on the grill. Just mix up your favorite recipe and either wrap it in foil or put it into an aluminum tray that you cover with aluminum foil. Your dressing will be done in 30 minutes, so you can be preparing that while your turkey starts to cook.

Grilled Turkey

Don't be tempted to peek at the turkey during the first hour to hour and a half. Lifting the lid causes heat to escape and can add another 15 minutes to the time it will take the turkey to get done. It's more fun checking during the last half (while you baste it), anyhow; the aroma just keeps getting better and better.

> One 9- to 12-pound turkey
> Salt
> Cooking oil
> Butter

1. Rinse turkey and pat dry with paper towels. Sprinkle some salt inside of the cavity. Skewer neck skin to the back, tie the legs to the tail, and twist wing tips under back. Rub the entire turkey with cooking oil. Insert a meat thermometer into the center of the inside thigh muscle, not touching the bone.

2 In a covered charcoal grill, arrange preheated coals around a large drip pan. (Use the indirect method on a gas grill.) You'll use a medium heat. Pour 1 inch of water into the drip pan. Place unstuffed bird, breast side up, on the grill rack above the drip pan but not over the coals.

3 Lower lid and grill for 2^1/$_2$ to 3 hours or until meat thermometer registers 180°F to 185°F, brushing occasionally with butter during the last half of the cooking time. If you're using a charcoal grill, add additional coals, if necessary; in most cases, the coals will last for 3 hours. Add water to the drip pan every 20 to 30 minutes or as necessary.

IF YOU'RE SO
INCLINED

For a "sorta" stuffing to go with the turkey, put some cubed potatoes in an oiled, grill-safe covered skillet on the grill shelf during the last hour of turkey grilling time. While the turkey rests before you carve it, move the pan to a hotter part of the grill and push the potatoes to one side. Add oil and sauté a chopped onion. Stir in dried bread cubes and scramble a couple of beaten eggs over top of the mixture. Stir frequently and season with salt and pepper.

Don't be tempted to taste your turkey too soon. After you take it off of the grill, wait 15 minutes before you carve it. It'll be juicier if you do.

Type A Behavior Turkey

Don't wanna wait 3 hours for your turkey to get done? Then follow these microwave precooking directions.

1 Follow the instructions given above for Grilled Turkey through Step 1.

2 Place the turkey breast side down in a microwave-safe dish. Cover the wing tips and legs with small pieces of foil if you can use foil in your microwave. Then cover the entire turkey with a tent of waxed paper and microwave on high for $1^1/2$ minutes. Turn the dish a half turn and microwave on high for another $1^1/2$ minutes.

3 Turn the turkey to breast side up and brush with more cooking oil. Microwave on high for $1^1/2$ minutes per pound, turning the dish halfway through that cooking time.

4 Insert a meat thermometer and continue to microwave on high until the temperature registers 140°F.

5 Transfer the turkey to the grill, breast side up, and grill according to Step 3 for the Grilled Turkey instructions above, except that it should only take about an hour for the turkey to reach the desired temperature of 185°F.

Wood-Smoked Turkey

Again, it's your call. Choose the type of wood you prefer: hickory, cherry, alder, or mesquite. Any of them will give your turkey a wonderful smoky taste and a bird grilled to a rich mahogany color.

1 Follow the instructions given above for Grilled Turkey through Step 1.

2 In a charcoal grill, such as the high-domed one from Weber, place a drip pan in the center under the rack. Place a generous amount of coals around the drip pan. Light the fire, and once the embers are thoroughly gray, put the wood chips you've first soaked in water for several minutes directly on top of the coals.

3 Fill the drip tray three-quarters full of water. (This is what helps keep the meat moist, so don't skip this step.) Place the turkey in the center of the rack, breast side up. Cover the grill with the lid, with all of the vents open. Smoke the turkey for 3 to 3^1/$_2$ hours, checking periodically to baste with butter and move the bird around enough so that it browns evenly. Add additional coals, if necessary, and be sure you don't let the drip pan go dry. Make sure it always has water.

4 The preferred serving method for smoked turkey is to let it cool and then refrigerate it until you're ready to enjoy your meal.

IF YOU'RE SO INCLINED

Tired of smoked wood flavor? Soak eight Earl Grey tea bags, 16 whole cloves, and four cinnamon sticks in water for 15 minutes. Cut four double-thickness sections of foil longer than the cinnamon sticks. Shape foil and place 2 tablespoons of water in each. Add 2 tablespoons uncooked brown rice to each. Open two teabags and sprinkle contents into each. Divide the other ingredients between the packets and fold closed. Prick pin holes in top of each packet and place directly onto the coals, at north, south, east, and west.

Getting Time on Your Side

	The Old Way	The Lazy Way
Chasing your main entrée	30 minutes	0 minutes
Tracking punny names for your recipes	15 minutes	0 minutes (you now have Mousse and Squirrel)
Brown bagging barbecue sauce	30 minutes (includes that trip to the store)	0 minutes (you catch on and start keeping extra of The Swiss Army Knife Equivalent of Barbecue Sauces on hand)
Camouflaging your food	60 minutes (making cute little costumes for your entrée, or sometimes a heavy sauce, to distract finicky eaters so they don't ask what's on their plates)	0 minutes (because you now know how to complement foods so you get compli-ments, too)
Stalking the wild strawberry	30 minutes	0 minutes (because you stock up on all natural preserves)
Howling at the moon	30 minutes (as part of your nightly stress-management program)	0 minutes (because you're mastering The Lazy Way)

twelve

Take Another Pizza My Heart!

While we certainly don't believe cooking is an exact science—after all, we've yet to meet the recipe we can't…er, in our humble opinions…improve—nowhere is that more evident than when it comes to grilling pizza. This does take some experimentation. You'll need to know the quirks…er, individual personality…of your grill and then adjust your cooking times accordingly. However, once you and your grill start talking in the same language, you'll be amazed that you ever even considered baking your creations which now seem so perfectly suited for the grill.

The easiest way to accomplish that task is to first understand a few pizza creation options. After that, simply pick the one that seems easiest (think: lazy equals efficient) and chances are that's what will work best for you. The possibilities are limited only by your pantry and your imagination.

A PERFECT FOUNDATION IS A CRUST

The wise man built his house upon the rock. Consider your pizza crust your Gibraltar, and let the construction begin!

The Dough

Makes four 8- to 10-inch pizza rounds

1 cup lukewarm water (105°F to 115°F)

1 tablespoon sugar

1 envelope dry yeast

3 tablespoons olive oil

3 cups (or more) all purpose flour (bread flour is okay, too)

$1^1/_2$ teaspoons salt

1(a) Food Processor Method

1 In processor, combine water and sugar. Sprinkle with yeast and let stand until foamy, about 10 minutes. Add oil, then 3 cups of flour and salt. Process until dough comes together, about 1 minute. Knead dough for 2 minutes or until it is smooth and elastic, adding more flour by the tablespoon if dough is sticky.

1(b) Breadmaker Method

1 Add all ingredients to breadmaker in order, according to the manufacturer's user manual. Set breadmaker on dough setting.

1(c)   Mixer Method

1 In the bowl of a stand mixer fitted with a dough hook, mix the water, sugar, and yeast. Let this stand until yeast is foamy. Add the salt and oil to the bowl and mix well. With the mixer on low speed, add the flour to the bowl and mix until all the flour is absorbed and the dough pulls away from the side of the bowl, adding additional flour a tablespoon at a time, if necessary.

1(d)   Mix by Hand Method

1 In a large bowl, stir together water, yeast, and sugar and let stand until foamy. Stir in remaining ingredients and blend until mixture forms a dough. Knead dough on a floured surface for 5 to 10 minutes, until it is smooth and elastic. Sprinkle the dough with additional flour a tablespoon at a time as necessary to prevent dough from sticking during the kneading process.

2 Lightly oil large bowl, add dough and turn it to coat with oil. Cover bowl with plastic wrap or a cotton or linen towel. Let stand in warm draft-free area until dough doubles, about 1 hour.

3 Punch down and then knead the dough in the bowl until smooth, about 2 minutes.

4 Next, divide it into 4 equal portions, shaping each into a ball. Place each dough round onto an oiled baking pan, or dust bottom portion with flour and leave near your floured crust-rolling area.

5 Brush the tops lightly with olive oil and cover with plastic wrap or dust them with flour and cover with a lightweight towel. (You can store the dough after portioning for 1 day in the refrigerator, but you must let it sit at room temperature for 1 hour before using.)

IF YOU'RE SO
INCLINED

Some pizza gourmets swear by using kosher salt in their dough. Kosher salt doesn't have the chemical preservatives and additives in some types. Sea salt is another popular choice. The choice is yours.

Keep your cool and move your picnic table into the shade (so you won't run the risk of sun-baking the tops of your dough rounds instead of allowing them to rise), and you can roll your pizza dough outside. Use a plastic cutting board or piece of plywood covered with cotton duck cloth large enough to roll out a round. Keep a small bowl of flour close by to dust the cutting board or cloth.

Once your dough rounds have raised again for up to an hour, you're ready to roll them out for grilling. On a lightly floured surface roll out 1 ball of dough until it is about $\frac{1}{8}$-inch thick or up to 10 inches in diameter. Now you're again faced with several options, which are:

1. If you're making your crust in advance of when you intend to grill your pizza, brush off the excess flour, transfer dough with your hands to an oiled baking sheet, and cover surface completely with plastic wrap. Repeat procedure with remaining dough balls and plastic wrap in same manner, stacking rolled-out pieces on top of one another on baking sheet. Wrap baking sheet with more plastic wrap to ensure that dough is completely covered. Chill dough until firm, about 1 hour, or freeze until needed.

2. If you're ready to fix your pizza now, you can either transfer a 10-inch round of dough to an oiled pan or, if the dough is firm enough—meaning it won't ooze its way onto your coals, flavor bar, or lava rock—place it directly on the oiled grid to your grill. Grill for 1 to 3 minutes and then flip over and add your toppings to the grilled side. (Grilling time will depend on the amount of toppings you intend to use. Thicker layers of toppings require longer grilling times during this step, so you'll grill for a shorter amount of time before you flip over the crust. Refer to the pizza varieties later in this chapter for more information on grilling times.)

3. If you prefer to grill your crust directly on the grid but you're concerned that the dough may not be

firm enough to do so, you can transfer it to an oiled pan and place it in the freezer for 15 minutes. Then place the crust directly on the grid and follow the steps explained in Step 2 above.

GETTING THINGS ALL FIRED UP: READYING THE GRILL

Regardless of the fuel you use, you'll get the best results using a covered grill. If your grill doesn't have a cover on hinges, don't despair. You can achieve similar results by creating an aluminum foil tent and using it to "shelter" your pizza.

Experienced pizza grilling gourmets swear by an assembly line-type of process possible on a larger grilling surface. Using that method, you crisp one side of your crust over hot coals (direct method) and then flip the crust over to the other unlit side of the grill to warm the toppings and melt the cheeses (indirect method).

Other grilling options include:

- To cook pizzas on a charcoal grill, build a medium-hot fire in one half of the grill. Two bricks can be placed end-to-end to serve as a divider.

- For a gas grill with two burners, preheat one burner on high and leave the other burner unlit.

- For a single-burner gas grill, first preheat on high, then lower the flame to medium and then to low to cook the second side of the pizza. (You can experiment with this. If your grill allows for your shelf to be at least 4 to 6 inches from your lava rock or

A COMPLETE WASTE OF TIME

The 3 Worst Things to Do When Making Pizza:

1. Omit salt from your crust recipe. Include at least a pinch for flavor enhancement.

2. Use water that is too hot—you will kill the yeast. (Cool overhot water by rapidly stirring in the sugar until it dissolves.)

3. Not let the children participate. (If you don't have any of your own handy, invite that kid riding by on her bicycle!)

flavor bars, you should be able to do all of your pizza grilling on medium.)

- Those of you who can afford a three-burner gas grill are on your own. Hire a consultant if you have any questions. (Or, if you've forgiven us for the above remarks, alternate between the direct and indirect grilling methods, according to your personal preferences.)

INTERROGATION TECHNIQUES: GRILLING OPTIONS FOR CRUSTS

Variety is the spice of life. And nowhere is that more evident than when it comes to the number of ways you can use a crust.

1. Place a dough round you've first pricked with a fork directly on the grid. Grill over medium heat until the top of the dough puffs and the underside is crisp, about 3 minutes. Flip and either grill for another minute or transfer to a baking sheet, well-grilled side up, and add your toppings. Repeat with remaining dough rounds.

2. When complete, form crusts on pizza pans, cover and let rise again. Prick dough with a fork so that air can escape during grilling. Grill 2 to 3 minutes per side until light brown.

If you don't intend to use the crusts right away, allow them to cool. Then wrap them tightly in foil and freeze until you get the pizza urge. These are handy for easy last minute dinners or when unexpected guests arrive at your door. Push those guests out the back door and seat them at the picnic table (and outside of your messy...er, lived in...house) until you're ready to serve the meal. If you want to go all out and be an exceptional host, you might offer them something to drink while they wait. This, of course, depends on how long you want them to stick around. Serve a salty anchovy pizza and they'll soon leave in search of something to satisfy their thirst.

A COMPLETE WASTE OF TIME

The 3 Worst Things to Do Before Grilling Your Pizza:

1. Forget to oil your pan or the hot grid to prevent your pizza from sticking.

2. Forget to preheat your grill.

3. Forget to make certain you have enough fuel (propane tank filled, plenty of charcoal or wood) on hand to complete your meal.

Use leftover gravy in place of pizza sauce. Or perhaps top the rice crust with pizza sauce, pepperoni, and mozzarella cheese. Onion and green pepper taste great, too—sauté first or add 'em raw so they stay a bit crunchy. Consider serving with Tabasco for extra zing!

The Price Is Rice Pizza

Don't limit your pizza crust options to those made from dough or French bread. Here's one way to use up that leftover rice and serve pizza in the process.

3 cups cooked rice (brown or white)

2 eggs

1 cup mozzarella cheese, grated

Dash salt and pepper

$1/2$ teaspoon dry mustard

$1^1/2$ tablespoons butter

3 tablespoons flour

$1^1/2$ cups milk

1 chicken bouillon cube crushed or
$1/2$ teaspoon of chicken soup base (Minor's or Redi-Base)

$1/2$ teaspoon oregano

$1/2$ teaspoon basil

$1/4$ teaspoon garlic powder

2 cups leftover cooked vegetables, such as broccoli or 1 cup cooked chicken and 1 cup vegetables

1 cup grated cheddar cheese

1. In a glass bowl, mix rice, eggs, mozzarella cheese, salt, pepper, and dry mustard together thoroughly. Spread the mixture onto an oiled 10×15-inch cookie sheet. Grill on low for 10 minutes or until eggs are set. Remove from grill until sauce is ready.

2. To prepare the sauce, place a cast-iron skillet over medium to high heat and melt the butter. Mix in the flour with a whisk or a fork. Add milk and stir until thickened and

smooth. Mix in the crushed chicken bouillon cube or the chicken soup base. Next add the oregano, basil, and garlic powder. Remove from heat and spoon over crust.

3 Spread the vegetables or chicken and vegetables on the sauce and top with the grated cheddar cheese.

4 Grill over low heat or indirect heat for 15 to 25 minutes, or until cheese topping is melted and bubbling.

QUICK ⬤ PAINLESS

For a quick crust, spread leftover mashed potatoes onto an oiled pizza pan. Add sauce and your choice of toppings and grill.

Keep extra tomato sauce on hand should the urge for a thicker, zestier sauce take hold of your inner being without warning. Simply add a little more than a recipe calls for to satisfy the urge.

HITTING THE SAUCE

Your sauce choices are as varied as the toppings you can layer on your pizza. With all of the recipes listed below, serving amounts depend on how much sauce you prefer on each pizza.

Now, get ready to think versatility!

The Kind Everybody Recognizes Pizza Sauce

This sauce works for either thick- or thin-crust pizza. If you prefer a thicker, zestier sauce, add more tomato paste. (Buying the kind in the tube comes in handy for just that sort of thing.)

  1 tablespoon olive oil
  One 28-ounce can plum tomatoes
  2 tablespoons tomato paste
  2 cloves garlic
  1 small onion
  1 1/4 teaspoons basil
  1/4 teaspoon salt
  1/4 teaspoon black pepper
  1/2 teaspoon sugar
  1/2 teaspoon oregano
  1/4 teaspoon red pepper flakes

1   Place a heavy saucepan on the grill. Once it's heated a bit, add the olive oil and be certain it coats the entire bottom of the pan. (This prevents the sauce from sticking.)

2 If you desire a milder sauce, mince the garlic and chop the onion and sauté them in the olive oil before adding the other ingredients. Otherwise, mix the crushed plum tomatoes, tomato paste, minced or crushed garlic, chopped onion, basil, salt, black pepper, sugar, oregano, and red pepper flakes in the saucepan and simmer until sauce reduces to desired consistency.

QUICK PAINLESS

In a hurry? Consider using dried minced garlic and onion in your sauce and simmer until they're tender.

Land o' Lakes makes a fat-free half and half. Another option is to substitute cottage cheese. If you fear it will be too moist, drain in a coffee filter-lined colander and then purée in the blender before adding to the Alfredo sauce. Should the sauce separate while you're heating it, add cornstarch or arrowroot in $1/2$ teaspoon increments until the sauce thickens.

"Who Is Alfredo and Why Is He Sauced?" Alfredo Sauce

Nowhere is it written that pizza sauce always has to be red. Give it a chance and this pasta classic will soon become one of your pizza favorites, too.

3 tablespoons butter

2 cloves garlic

2 heaping tablespoons flour

1 pint half & half or heavy whipping cream

Bunch fresh parsley

$1/3$ cup grated parmesan cheese

1   In a heavy saucepan or cast-iron skillet, melt butter over medium-low heat. Mince the garlic and sauté in the butter for 2 to 3 minutes. Stir in flour to create a roux and then gradually add half & half, stirring constantly.

2   Coarsely chop parsley to make $1/4$ cup.

3   Once the sauce is heated through and thickened, add the parmesan cheese and parsley.

Another Alfredo (But No Relation) Sauce

Choices are good. There's more than one way to get sauced. And there's more than one Alfredo, too. Feel free to substitute cottage cheese for the ricotta; you don't even have to drain it first because the cornstarch will keep it from going watery on you.

1 clove garlic

1 tablespoon butter

$^1/_4$ cup part-skim ricotta cheese

$^1/_4$ cup plain yogurt

$^1/_4$ cup grated Parmesan cheese

Optional: $^1/_2$ to 1 teaspoon cornstarch

Optional: $^1/_4$ teaspoon white pepper

Optional: $^1/_4$ teaspoon oregano

Optional: $^1/_4$ teaspoon basil

Optional: $^1/_4$ teaspoon parsley flakes

1 In a heavy saucepan or cast-iron skillet, melt butter over medium-low heat. Mince the garlic and sauté in the butter for 2 to 3 minutes. Stir in the ricotta cheese, yogurt, and Parmesan cheese.

2 Some yogurts can separate during the heating process. If so, stir in enough cornstarch to thicken the sauce and stir until well-blended.

3 After sauce is heated through, add the white pepper and other optional herbs if you wish.

YOU'LL THANK YOURSELF LATER

Why not make your own "special" Alfredo sauce by adding some secret ingredients to impress your guests. (Forget trying to impress your family!) Consider trying alternatives, such as deglazing the pan with a splash of white wine (after you've sautéed the garlic) or adding some cayenne pepper or onion powder.

Some fireside chefs prefer to sauté garlic in olive oil instead of butter. Another way to add a change-of-pace taste to your sauce is to sauté the garlic a bit longer than usual, until it has a nutty aroma and is golden brown.

Pep Up Your Pizza Red Pepper Sauce

Roasted red peppers are truly one of life's food pleasures. You'll please your palate with this recipe.

1 clove garlic

$^{1}/_{4}$ teaspoon salt

6 ounces roasted red peppers

1 tablespoon tomato paste

Freshly ground black pepper to taste

1 In a bowl, use the back of a spoon to mash garlic and salt into a paste.

2 Move the garlic and salt paste to a blender or food processor and then add roasted red peppers (See Chapter 13 for instructions on how to roast red peppers) and tomato paste. Add black pepper to taste. Puree until smooth.

Serving suggestion: Use this sauce on a pizza that you top with one 6$^{1}/_{2}$-ounce can solid white tuna in water, drained and flaked, 2 tablespoons drained capers, 2 red onions sliced into $^{1}/_{4}$-inch-thick rings and grilled, and another 6 ounces of chopped roasted red peppers that have been tossed in 1$^{1}/_{2}$ tablespoons of extra-virgin olive oil, 3 tablespoons fresh lemon juice, $^{1}/_{2}$ teaspoon thyme, $^{1}/_{4}$ teaspoon salt, and 1 crushed garlic clove.

SOME ASSEMBLY REQUIRED: PIZZA POSSIBILITIES

The choice is yours. You can stick with topping your pizza with the same ol', same ol' available from the local pizzeria. Or you can choose the quick and efficient way to impress your friends by trying these suggested combinations:

Lemon-Pepper Pleaser

Add 2 teaspoons of lemon zest and 1 teaspoon of cracked black pepper to your crust recipe. This makes a crust ideal for eggplant caviar or a seafood topping.

Color Cascade Pizza

Layer the pizza in this order: pizza sauce, finely grated mozzarella cheese, spinach, chopped red bell peppers, fresh mushrooms, and (optional) feta cheese.

Roasted Garlic and Rosemary Razzmatazz

Add 6 diced cloves of roasted garlic and 2 teaspoons of fresh rosemary (or $^2/_3$ teaspoon of dried rosemary, first soaked in some water for an hour, then drained and dried) to your crust recipe. This one is perfect for a pizza made using Alfredo sauce and topped with grilled chicken, black olives, sliced fresh mushrooms, steamed broccoli, and grated romano, parmesan, and mozzarella cheeses.

Pizza Carbonara

Some claim that carbonara sauce was invented by charcoal workers to sustain them while working on the slopes of the Apennines. Others say that the generous layer of black pepper sprinkled over the pasta dish looks like

QUICK 🆖 PAINLESS

No time to roast red peppers? You have two options: (1) Drain and rinse a jar of red peppers, or (2) use the appropriate amount of a product such as Minor's Roasted Red Bell Pepper Concentrate. (Refer to Appendix A, "How To Get Someone Else To Do It," for suggestions on this and other products.)

charcoal dust and hence the name. Regardless of its origins, you can create a carbonara-style pizza by adding a beaten egg to each pizza-sized portion of the cottage cheese-style Alfredo sauce. Top your pizza with crispy pieces of bacon, onion, mozzarella cheese, and, of course, freshly ground black pepper.

Stuffed Crust Special

When it comes to what you use to stuff the crust, the choice is yours: cheese, meat, veggies, or a combination of all three. To make certain that your crust "bakes" completely on the grill, think omelet...sort of.

Generously coat a cookie sheet with olive oil. Combine two pizza rounds and roll that amount of dough out until it's not only very thin, but so that it's a rectangle that fits the cookie sheet, too. Dust off extra flour and place on the cookie sheet. Prick the dough with a fork. Grill for about 3 minutes, or until some air bubbles form on the upper crust. The crust will need to be firm enough for you to flip it over on the cookie sheet.

After you've done that, add your "stuffings" to half of the crust, keeping them close to the center. Fold the crust over and secure edges by pressing with a fork. Grill for another 3 minutes. Flip the crust over again. Add your toppings and return to the grill until the cheese melts and bubbles.

Instead of Pizza Sauce

Don't get stuck in a rut! Who says pizza always needs a red sauce? Open up your world using one of these suggestions:

- Think about substituting a generous layer of garlic butter instead.

- Another tasty possibility is using one of your favorite vinaigrette dressings, such as $1/8$ cup of extra-virgin olive oil, 1 tablespoon of balsamic vinegar, 1 clove of crushed garlic, and $1/3$ teaspoon rosemary.

- You can even use a homemade or commercial salad dressing, such as Ranch or Italian, to complement the appropriate toppings.

- We're still not done! Grab your favorite barbecue sauce and spread some across the crust. This makes a great complement for a ham-and-pineapple-chunk pizza.

Very Veggie-tarian Varieties

Just as there's more than one type of sauce for your pizza, there are also other mushroom varieties besides the standard white button type. We're including a recipe for portabello mushrooms to showcase one alternative.

Grilled Portabello Mushroom and Eggplant Feast

Mix 1 crushed clove garlic together with a tablespoon of olive oil and use to coat 4 sliced portabello mushrooms and 20 eggplant slices; grill the vegetables for 2 minutes each side. Brush the crust with the remaining garlic and olive oil. Top with 2 cups of grated mozzarella cheese and the mushroom and eggplant slices, followed by $1/2$ cup of grated parmesan, and grill until cheeses melt.

Congratulations! You've discovered a way to get your kids to eat their veggies. When you serve them pizza-style, they probably won't even notice that they're eating healthy.

The Lazy Way

For deep-dish or other styles of pan pizza, ensure your topping will warm completely by grilling the pizza in two steps. Cover your pizza with half the toppings. Grill 3 to 5 minutes or until the cheeses melt. Add remaining ingredients and repeat. The thicker your crust, the longer you'll need to "prebake" your topping side of the crust before you pile on the goodies and cheeses.

Use That Extra Crust Salad Pizza

The next time you fix pizza, grill an extra crust until done. Refrigerate and before serving, top with a thin layer of mayonnaise and 4 to 8 ounces of softened cream cheese. You can either add a layer of chopped raw vegetables and 1 cup of grated cheddar cheese or top with raw or roasted vegetables that have been marinated overnight in balsamic vinegar and extra-virgin olive oil, or lemon juice and extra-virgin olive oil.

Dessert Pizza

We include even more pizza recipes elsewhere in this book. Check out Chapter 15 for some dessert pizza creations.

PERSONAL PECCADILLOES

Now that you know the proper way to create your pizza, let Pam show you how she makes hers.

Pam's Breaking All of the Rules But It Works Pizza Crust

One time, when a friend asked for her pizza recipe, Pam used "some" as the measurement for most of the ingredients. (When she mentioned the amount of sugar, she told the friend "not as much as some of this 'some'" so she'd be sure to use a higher ratio of flour.) Pam believes it's important to keep in mind that this is another one of those situations where you first have to know the rules before you can break them. This started out as Pam's means to make homemade crusts whenever she only had enough time to do so in a hurry. With practice, the method evolved to where she would intuitively know the amounts of flour to use by the "feel" of the dough. It's now her family's preferred method for making crusts. Keep in mind that this method makes a crust you'll definitely need to either grill on a pan or pre-freeze to make it firm enough to place directly on the grid.

Makes four 8- to 10-inch pizza rounds

1 cup hot water

$^1/_8$ cup (4 tablespoons) sugar

$2^1/_4$ teaspoons dry yeast powder

1 teaspoon salt

1 tablespoon olive oil

2 cups flour (plus up to 1 additional cup)

1   Here's the method Pam uses to get the water temperature to the perfect bubble-up-the-yeast state: Run water at the faucet until it reaches its hottest temperature and measure out a cup. Slowly pour that water into a glass or plastic bowl large enough to hold all of the ingredients. Add the sugar and stir until the sugar dissolves. Add the dry yeast powder and stir enough to dampen the yeast. Let the mixture sit for 5 to 15 minutes so the yeast begins to form a foam on top.

2   Once the yeast and sugar water mixture begins to bubble (and not before), add the salt and olive oil. Dump in the entire 2 cups of flour and use a fork to mix, going against all you've been told about making yeast bread recipes and being careful not to overmix the ingredients. At this point, you should be able to pull the mixture from the sides of the

YOU'LL THANK YOURSELF LATER

You can expand the "shelf life" of yeast by storing it in the refrigerator.

bowl so that it forms a large ball. If it is too moist to do this, dust over-moist areas with a tablespoon of flour, moving the dough ball around in the bowl enough to coat the mixture with the flour.

3 Dump $1/2$ cup of flour onto your table or rolling area and spread it around until it's the circumference of your dough. Dump the ball of dough out of the bowl and into the middle of that flour. Pour a tablespoon of flour into the palm of one hand and then rub your hands together over the dough so that the flour dusts the top of the dough and coats your hands. (Remember, this mixture is a bit more moist than you're probably used to working with, so you'll need to be careful until you get the hang of it and feel your way around at first.)

4 Pour 4 tablespoons of flour onto the table in 4 even piles; this is where you're going to put your dough rounds. Carefully roll the dough in the flour on the table until it's coated and then pinch off a fourth of the dough, again coating it with flour if it seems too moist, and form it into a ball and set it in one of the tablespoon-sized mounds of flour. Repeat 3 more times until you have 4 equal sections of dough.

5 Depending on the warmth of your room, you only need let the 4 dough rounds rise for 5 to 15 minutes! They won't double in that time, of course; they'll just feel a bit, shall we say, punchier. (That's the official term!) Pick up the punchiest dough round first and move it back to the original floured area. Dust the top with flour. Press it down into a flat round and then, using a rolling pin (with a very light touch! Press too hard and it'll stick to the table), roll the dough until you have an 8- to 10-inch pizza dough about $1/8$-inch thick.

6 Brush off excess flour and move the dough to a baking sheet that will fit on your grill. Use a fork to punch a few holes in the crust. Grill for 2 to 3 minutes per side and move to a rack while you prebake the remaining crusts. Once you prebake the crusts, they can be placed directly on the grill when you add your choice of toppings. (Then you'll grill anywhere from 3 to 10 minutes, depending on the amount of toppings.)

A Crustimonial: It really does take longer to describe how to prepare this crust than it takes to actually make it. Once you get the hang of it, you'll love it. Pam tried an experiment recently to confirm just how easy it is to make these crusts come out right. She had her grand-daughter, Taylor (3 years, 2 months, and 17 days old at the time), measure (with 3-year-old accuracy), add, and then stir all of the ingredients. "Gramma" then divided the dough into the 4 segments, but Taylor coated them with flour and made the "rounds," repeatedly counted to 10 until it was time to roll them out, and then rolled out the crusts herself. Gramma just had to dust off the extra flour and move the crusts to the pan to grill them. Keep in mind that it's now a tradition at Pam's house to tear off chunks of the first crust and eat it with butter, so plan accordingly.

Congratulations! By now you have enough sauce and crusts on hand to be ready to feed any hungry horde.

The Lazy Way

Pam's Sweet As She (Modestly) Is Pizza Sauce

This makes enough sauce for a bunch of pizzas! Of course, the number in your bunch will depend on whether or not you like as much sauce on your pizza as we do. This sauce only keeps for about two weeks in the refrigerator, so freeze the extra.

Makes 4^1/$_2$ cups

1 tablespoon olive oil

One 29-ounce can of tomato puree (we prefer Contadina)

1 cup water

^{1}/$_8$ cup plus 1 tablespoon (5 tablespoons) sugar

1^1/$_2$ to 2 teaspoons salt

1 tablespoon garlic powder

1 tablespoon dried onion flakes or minced onion

2 teaspoons oregano

1 Heat a heavy saucepan on the burner until warm and add the olive oil, turning the pan to coat the bottom. (This helps keep the sauce from sticking.) Add the tomato puree, then dump water into that can, swoosh it a bit to rinse out the rest of the puree, and pour it into the saucepan. Reduce heat to low and add sugar, salt, garlic, onion, and oregano.

2 Simmer over low heat for an hour, stirring occasionally to verify the sauce isn't sticking to the bottom of the pan or scorching. Spoon onto the pizza crust and add toppings.

Getting Time on Your Side

	The Old Way	The Lazy Way
Looking up the phone number for pizza delivery	5 minutes	0 minutes
Calling the pizza delivery and waiting on hold	10 minutes	0 minutes
Hanging up from pizza delivery to go find coupons	1 minute	0 minutes
Hunting for coupons	15 minutes	0 minutes
Redialing pizza delivery, waiting on hold, and ordering pizza	10 minutes	0 minutes
Waiting for the pizza delivery to arrive	30 minutes (or less, but you still have to spend that time hunting down change or small bills for the tip)	0 minutes

A Lucky Number for Vegetable Grilling

While you can still use your grill to satisfy your plebian tastes for a generic cookout of hamburgers and hot dogs, if we've taught you nothing else in this book, it should be an appreciation that if you stop there, you're missing out on a lot.

We'll cover some cast-iron skillet vegetable grilling options in Chapter 16, "The Whole Shebang—Entire Meals on the Grill," and during a discussion of kabobs in Chapter 14. In this chapter, we're primarily concerned with the following two vegetable grilling options: foil-wrapped packets and slices large enough to grill directly on the grid.

Soon you'll have everyone thinking that veggies are our friends. Because whichever method you use to prepare them, we're convinced you'll find that grilling not only retains the nutritional value, but it makes already great vegetable flavors taste even better.

QUICK ⬤ PAINLESS

Vegetable Grilling Methods

Vegetable	Foil	On Grill
Beets	X	
Cabbage	X	
Carrots	X	
Cucumbers	X	
Eggplant*	X	X
Fennel	X	X
Onions	X	X
Parsnips	X	
Peppers*	X	X
Potatoes	X	
Rutabagas	X	
Summer Squash	X	X
Tomatoes	X	X
Turnips	X	
Winter Squash	X	

* indicates another alternative grilling method or special instruction for these vegetables

TO FOIL OR NOT TO FOIL, PLEASE USE DISCRETION

Some grilling purists consider using foil packets as "simply steaming" food and don't appreciate the all-around ease of that method—less cleanup involved, no worries of smaller veggies falling through the rack, etc. True, vegetables grilled directly on the rack will absorb more of that smoky, rich, outdoor-cooking flavor. But we'll give you some foil packet hints that let you combine the best of both worlds.

Foil Packet Grilling Directions

Cut an 18-inch square of heavy-duty aluminum foil. Place vegetable in center of the foil. Season to taste with salt and pepper. Dot with butter and coat with an infused olive oil (see Chapter 4, "Sanity-Saving Shortcuts and Tried 'n' True Tips"), or add 1 tablespoon water or broth. Bring up the two opposite edges of foil, leaving some space for expansion of steam. Roll the foil to tightly seal the top of the packet and then seal each end in the same way. Place the foil packet on cooking grate. Cook over indirect heat for the time given in the following chart, turning packet over once halfway through grilling time. The times given are for crisp-tender vegetables, but if you prefer tender vegetables, just cook longer.

YOU'LL THANK YOURSELF LATER

Wrap unpeeled beets in foil and roast on the grill. You can easily slip off the skin once the beets are cool and avoid messy purple-stained fingers in the process.

Cooking Times

Foil-wrapped Vegetables	Amount	Estimated Cooking Time
Beans, green and wax (whole)	1 cup	30 to 35 minutes
Beets, small whole	$1^1/_2$ cups	30 to 60 minutes
Broccoli flowerets	1 cup	15 to 18 minutes
Brussels sprouts	$1^1/_2$ cups	18 to 20 minutes
Cabbage	$1^1/_2$ cups	20 to 25 minutes
Carrots ($1/_2$-inch slices)	$1^1/_2$ cups	15 to 20 minutes
Cauliflower flowerets	2 cups	20 to 25 minutes
Corn on the cob*	4 medium ears	25 to 35 minutes
Eggplant* (1-inch slices)	1 small	20 to 25 minutes
Kohlrabi (julienne strips)	$1^1/_2$ cups	25 to 30 minutes
Mushrooms (whole or sliced)	$1^1/_2$ cups	8 to 12 minutes
Peppers (1-inch strips), sweet red, green, or yellow	$1^1/_2$ cups	15 to 20 minutes
Potatoes (foil-wrapped)	4 medium	50 to 60 minutes
Yellow summer squash	$1^1/_2$ cups	6 to 10 minutes
Zucchini ($1/_2$-inch slices)	$1^1/_2$ cups	6 to 10 minutes

Potato Possibilities

Now that you have your potatoes sliced, diced, or quartered, before you seal up that foil packet, consider one of the following seasoning suggestions:

- Add butter and sliced shallots. The subtle garlic and onion distinction created from the shallots turns your ho-hum, humdrum potatoes into a dish that will convince your friends you truly are a gourmet chef!

- Add butter and sprinkle the potatoes with dill. Another pleasant, yet different, taste treat.

- Add olive oil and grill. Toss with a bit of extra virgin olive oil and sprinkle some balsamic vinegar over the potatoes before serving. Truly wonderful!

THE GRATE GRID METHOD

Large vegetables can be grilled directly on the cooking grate. Brush with oil and season with salt and pepper before placing them on the grill. Halve large tomatoes horizontally; slice squash lengthwise. Turn once during grilling.

IF YOU'RE SO
INCLINED

Speed up the cooking time for brussels sprouts by cutting a small X into the bottom of each one.

An earful of suggestions:

1. If you'd rather not turn the ears by hand during grilling, consider placing them in a vegetable holder such as one made by Weber.

2. Why settle for plain ol' butter when you can add minced garlic, chives, or other favorite herbs to make a hearty herbed butter that'll add distinct flavor to your corn.

3. Substitute an infused oil for butter.

Corn on the Grill

At least once a year, we make a meal of nothing but sweet corn and crusty chunks of homemade bread with butter. Roll the corn on the bread and then salt to taste. Delicious.

Servings vary

Sweet corn in the husk

Water

Optional: 1 cup sugar for each 12 ears of corn

1. For each ear of corn, peel back the husks enough to be able to remove the silk, then pull the husks back up and over the ear.

2. In a pan or bucket large enough to completely cover the corn with cold water, soak the ears for 20 minutes to an hour. (Some people swear by adding a little sugar to the water at this step. Use 1 cup of sugar for a dozen ears of corn.)

3. Grill the corn in the husks on the upper shelf over medium heat, turning every 5 minutes. Grill 20 minutes or until the corn is dark yellow in color and the husks are light to medium brown. If the husks dry out too much during this time and either look like they'll start burning or do ignite, sprinkle them with more water.

You MUST try this to believe it! Use lime juice and freshly grated black pepper on corn on the cob instead of butter. This heart-healthy suggestion gives corn a unique flavor that will make you wonder why you ever served it with butter.

Balsamic Eggplant

This recipe teaches you the secret to good eggplant. Whether you plan to use this marinade or simply intend to brush the eggplant with olive oil, always salt it first according to the directions in Step 1 below.

Makes 4 servings

1 large eggplant

1 cup balsamic vinegar

$^1/_2$ cup sugar

1 teaspoon parsley

1 teaspoon chives

1 teaspoon salt

$^1/_2$ teaspoon ground black pepper

$^1/_2$ cup light olive oil

1 Skin and slice the eggplant into $^1/_4$-inch-lengthwise slices. Salt and drain in a colander for a half hour. Rinse and pat dry.

2 In a glass bowl large enough to hold the marinade and the eggplant, combine the remaining ingredients. Marinate 4 hours or overnight.

3 Grill over medium heat for 5 minutes each side. The eggplant will appear dark brown and lightly crisp on the outside and will be soft in the center.

YOU'LL THANK YOURSELF LATER

Always grill cabbage on an upper rack over a low to medium grill. If the temperature is too high, it will cause the sulfur components in the cabbage to break down, which gives it a strong taste and smell.

Roasted garlic takes on a mild, nutty taste that is wonderful when spread onto crusty bread by itself or first mixed with some butter. (Plan on using an entire head of roasted or grilled garlic for each stick of butter.) You'll love both of these easy methods:

Option 1. Wrap unpeeled heads of garlic in heavy duty foil and place on upper shelf of grill. Roast for 35 minutes. Allow to cool and then squeeze the cloves out of the skin and into a small glass bowl. Mash the garlic and it's ready to serve or to add to butter.

Option 2. For each head of garlic, peel off the loose layers of skin, but don't expose the delicate flesh of the cloves. Shape heavy aluminum foil into a muffin-sized cup, one for each head of garlic. Put the garlic head in a foil. Drizzle with a tablespoon of olive oil. (Optional: Sprinkle with salt, pepper, thyme or rosemary.) Place the cups on the outer edge of the cooking grid. Close grill lid and cook over low heat for about an hour, drizzling twice more with olive oil. (If using an open grill, create a cover for each cup with a small piece of aluminum foil.) The cloves will feel quite mushy when ready.

The easiest way to store garlic is to make a garlic braid. Visit your favorite produce stand in late summer or early fall and buy 12 softneck bulbs with stems that are still flexible. Leave about a half inch of the roots on the bulbs, then lay three bulbs on a flat surface and braid the stems together several times. Work in each additional bulb by holding a new stem together with one of the other stems and continue to braid. Once you add the last

QUICK PAINLESS

A garlic braid, available in many produce departments, is the easiest way to store garlic. As long as you remember to hang it out of direct sunlight and away from moisture (such as steam from the stove or sink), you can snip off as much as you need, when you need it.

MASTER THE GRILL The Lazy Way

bulb, braid until you have at least 6 inches from which to make a hanging loop. Now, as long as you remember to hang the braid out of direct sunlight and away from moisture (such as steam from the stove or sink), you can snip off as much garlic as you need, whenever you need it.

A COMPLETE WASTE OF TIME

The 3 Worst Things to Do with Grilled Vegetables:

1. Parboil vegetables before grilling, which robs them of flavor. If you're short on time, precook them in a covered dish in the microwave.

2. Limit yourself to adding only oil, butter, or water to your foil packets. For example, marsala wine creates an interesting glaze for carrots; the alcohol cooks away and you're left with the delicate flavor enhancement.

3. Add too much of a good thing. When in doubt, start out using smaller amounts of an herb than the recipe calls for so you don't overpower the dish. You know your own tastes, so trust your judgment.

For a pucker-up pleasing, out-of-the-ordinary side dish, season grilled squash with some extra virgin olive oil and raspberry or strawberry wine vinegar.

Fiery Sweet Mushrooms

Perk up an ordinary meal with this extraordinary mushroom dish.

Makes 4 to 6 servings

1 pound fresh small button mushrooms

1 clove garlic

1 small green onion

Fresh ginger root

$1/3$ cup honey

$1/4$ cup white wine vinegar

$1/4$ cup dry white wine or vegetable broth

1 tablespoon soy sauce

1 teaspoon sesame oil

$1/2$ teaspoon grated orange peel

$1/4$ teaspoon ground red pepper

1   Clean the mushrooms, pat dry with paper towels, put into a glass bowl, and set aside.

2   Place a cast-iron skillet on the grill rack. Mince the garlic and chop the onion. Grate the ginger to make 1 teaspoon, and add to skillet along with the garlic, onion, honey, wine vinegar, white wine or broth, soy sauce, orange peel, and red pepper. Continue to cook until mixture is hot.

3   Pour mixture over the mushrooms. Stir to coat all of the mushrooms. Serve warm or refrigerate covered for 3 hours or longer to serve cold.

Optional: Use parsley springs and orange wedges for garnish.

Glorious Grilled Onions

One method for grilling onions is to peel them, cut 'em in half, brush 'em with oil, and grill 'em until they're charred on each side. That takes around 15 to 20 minutes. (You lightly scrape off the charred stuff before you serve them that way.) This is another alternative.

1 tablespoon balsamic or red wine vinegar

1 tablespoon water

1 tablespoon brown sugar

Dash of pepper

2 tablespoons vegetable oil

6 medium Bermuda or large yellow onions

1 Combine vinegar, water, brown sugar, pepper and oil in a bowl and mix well.

2 Halve unpeeled onions, cutting an X into the flat portion. Cut a large enough section from each of the unpeeled ends so that the onions will sit upright once they're grilled. Brush cut surfaces with the marinade.

3 Arrange onions, larger cut side down, on oiled grill and cook 5 to 6 inches above hot coals for 10 minutes. Turn over and brush again with the dressing. Continue to grill until the onions are crisp-tender and browned, or about another 10 to 15 minutes.

4 Stand onions upright with smaller cut side down to serve, opening them by pushing against the X cut so that they have an opened flower appearance.

YOU'LL THANK YOURSELF LATER

The easiest way to peel onions is to delegate. However, for those times when there isn't anyone else handy (or willing) to do it, cut the onion into quarters, then cut off the tiny portion at both ends of the resulting four pieces, and voilà! The peel now slides off easily.

Roasted Peppers

Our favorite is roasted red peppers. They're colorfully attractive and delicious. However, these instructions work for any peppers you have on hand, from run-of-the-mill green ones to the hot, hot varieties. (Just remember to wear rubber gloves and practice other "never touch your eyes"-type precautions when roasting habanero and other zesty varieties.)

1   Wash peppers.

2   Using a long-handled fork, char peppers over an open flame, turning them until skins are blackened, 2 to 8 minutes. Alternatively, grill whole peppers directly on the rack, turning them every 5 minutes, until skins are blistered and charred, 15 to 25 minutes.

3   Transfer peppers to a bowl and let stand, covered, until cool enough to handle. Or place peppers in a brown paper bag and seal the bag top, setting aside until peppers are cool.

4   Keeping peppers whole, peel them, starting at blossom end. Cut off tops and discard seeds and ribs. (Wear rubber gloves when handling chilies; be careful not to touch your face, especially around the eyes.)

IF YOU'RE SO
INCLINED

Once you're hooked, you'll never run out of uses for roasted red peppers. They're great in pasta and pizza sauce (see Chapter 12) or added to a sandwich or salad. It's a taste sensation you have to experience to believe!

Cheesy Herbed Tomato Grill

Fresh tomatoes, cheese, and your grill. Sheer delight. All this and heaven, too!

Makes 6 servings

3 large firm, ripe tomatoes

2 tablespoons olive oil

Salt and pepper to taste

1 teaspoon dried basil

1 tablespoon grated Parmesan cheese or more to taste

1 Wash tomatoes and cut them in half. Brush the six tomato sections with olive oil. Place them on the oiled grill, cut side down, 4 to 5 inches over hot fire, and grill 4 to 5 minutes.

2 Turn tomatoes using a wide spatula and sprinkle with salt, pepper, and basil.

3 Grate 1 tablespoon cheese and sprinkle on tomatoes.

4 Cook 4 to 5 minutes longer or until tomatoes are tender but still hold their shape. Remove from grill and serve hot or warm.

Tomato and basil are a match made in heaven. So, by all means, if you have basil growing in your herb garden, use it fresh. Use a half to a full teaspoon of chopped basil on each tomato half. Place some on the plate or serving platter as garnish, too.

Seasoned Simmering Summersations

This mixed vegetable combination is delicious served warm as a side dish or when chilled in the marinade for at least 4 hours and served with greens as a salad. Use a combination of vegetables you have on hand or those fresh from your garden. This dish lends itself to the type of fun meal preparation where the family can gather around the picnic table and help slice vegetables while the marinade simmers on the grill.

Makes 2 cups of marinade, Serves 4 to 8

Marinade

2 tablespoons olive oil

1 clove garlic

$1/4$ cup dry white wine

1 cup chicken stock

$1/4$ cup water

2 tablespoons lemon juice

$1/8$ teaspoon thyme

$1/4$ teaspoon parsley

$1/4$ teaspoon ground celery seed

$1/4$ teaspoon salt

4 peppercorns

Vegetables

Broccoli flowerets

Brussels sprouts

Carrots

IF YOU'RE SO
INCLINED

Keep bags of frozen vegetables on hand. Add them in place of fresh veggies and save yourself some chopping. You can get 100 percent lemon juice in your freezer case. We use the kind that comes in the neat yellow squirt bottle and we've yet to get a ticket from the cooking precision police!

Celery or fennel hearts or strips

Cucumbers

Cauliflower flowerets

Green beans

Tiny white onions

Sweet onion

Sugar snap peas

Small red potatoes

Summer squash (crookneck yellow, zucchini, etc.)

Turnips

Winter squash (acorn, butternut, etc.)

1   Place a deep cast-iron or other heavy skillet or Dutch oven over a medium grill. Once pan is heated, add the olive oil and allow time for the oil to come up to temperature, making certain it coats the entire bottom of the skillet. Add minced garlic and allow it to sauté for a minute or two.

2   Stir in the white wine (and then pause for a moment to savor the aroma as the wine deglazes the pan), chicken stock, water, and lemon juice. Add the thyme, parsley, ground celery seed, salt, and peppercorns. Simmer for 30 to 45 minutes, adjusting the grill temperature as necessary. (You do not want to boil this marinade…yet.)

3   NOW! After 30 to 45 minutes, increase the temperature of the grill or, if using charcoal, move the skillet to the area directly over the coals and bring marinade to a boil. Add your vegetables and simmer or poach until crisp tender (almost tender). Keep in mind that some veggies cook faster than others. Add the slower cooking ones first. Because you don't want to overcook any of your choices, you may need to fish some out with a slotted spoon and put them in your serving dish until the other veggies are done.

Slightly Skewered

We cover kabobs in Chapter 14, so check out those pages for even more ways to grill vegetables.

Getting Time on Your Side

	The Old Way	**The Lazy Way**
Turning your nose up at veggies	1 minute (or the time to pass the serving dish on to the person next to you)	0 minutes
Being a grilling snob about using foil packets	1,440 minutes a day	0 minutes
Tossing leftover veggies on the compost heap	5 minutes	0 minutes
Hanging pieces of foil (instead of unused AOL CDs) in your trees to scare away unwanted fruit-eating birds	60 minutes	0 minutes
Allowing your fear of zucchini surplus keep you from buying anything but flower seeds and plants	15 minutes	0 minutes
Wondering why nobody has come up with a feed the world population plan that uses all of that surplus zucchini	30 minutes	30 minutes (you can't win 'em all!)

Stab 'Em and Grab 'Em Finger Foods

When Mongol nomads took a break from their marauding and pillaging, they'd often spend time on the steppes of Asia Minor, roasting horse meat over their campfires. (Hey! Don't complain to us. We didn't pick out their main course!) The Turks called this meal *sis kebabi*, which literally means "sword meat." They threaded the horse meat onto their sabers. Since there aren't many opportunities in the marauding and swashbuckling departments anymore, most of us no longer carry a sword and we have to improvise.

Any shish kabob (sometimes spelled shish kebab) is made up of three components: the marinade, the meat, and the skewer. In an ideal world, the meat should be cut in uniformly-sized pieces. This ensures even cooking. This is also not the time to skimp on the fat; it's what absorbs the smoky flavor from the coals and it tenderizes the meat as it melts.

Of course, kabobs aren't always used as appetizers. The first recipe below can serve as a main course. However, because food prepared that way lends itself so well to what we think of as "pick-it-up-with-a-toothpick-or-our-fingers" food, we decided to include kabobs in the appetizers chapter. We'll start out with a kabob recipe, follow that up with some kabobbin' good suggestions, and then wrap up this chapter with lots of other appetizer ideas. En garde!

Tempting Teriyaki Kabobs

The addition of the green onions in this recipe not only adds flavor, it adds character to this appetizer's presentation.

- 1 pound beef sirloin steak or beef round steak, $1^1/4$ inches thick
- 2 bunches green onion (scallions)

Marinade

- $^1/4$ cup soy sauce
- $^1/4$ cup red wine vinegar
- $^1/4$ cup water
- 2 tablespoons honey
- $^1/4$ teaspoon garlic salt or garlic powder
- $^1/4$ teaspoon ground allspice
- $^1/8$ teaspoon ground ginger

1 Cut the meat into 1-inch strips. Then cut each strip into $^1/4$ inch pieces and cut an "X" in the center of each piece. (The "X" will make the meat easier to thread onto the onion, part of Step 3.)

IF YOU'RE SO
INCLINED

The Tempting Teriyaki Kabobs marinade can be used with chicken pieces if you omit the wine vinegar (or use a much smaller amount, if you prefer to retain some to enhance the flavor).

2   In a glass bowl large enough to hold all of the meat, mix the marinade. Add beef pieces and refrigerate 24 to 48 hours, using the longer marinating time for cheaper cuts of beef.

3   When ready to prepare for the grill, wash the green onions and trim away tops and roots. Thread an onion on each of your skewers. Then carefully thread the meat over the onion, leaving some space between each piece of meat.

4   Grill over hot coals, about 10 to 15 minutes, turning frequently.

A COMPLETE WASTE OF TIME

The 3 Worst Things to Do with Skewers:

1. Forget that metal skewers retain the heat for a *long* period of time after they're removed from the grill. Use appropriate caution so nobody gets burned.

2. Fail to soak wooden or bamboo skewers as suggested earlier. The only thing that should go up in smoke are your coals.

3. Think you can substitute great-granny's plastic knitting needles for skewers.

Add self-basting foods to your skewers. For example, thread bacon between chicken livers or pineapple chunks between some ham. The trick is to use foods that either require a similar grilling time or those, such as fruits, that are flexible enough to adapt to that required by their skewer mates.

SLIGHTLY SKEWERED

Your succulent kabobs will be an even bigger success if you remember these few tips:

- Leave spaces between the pieces of food when you thread them on skewers. Food will cook faster and more evenly when you do this.

- If you're using thin bamboo skewers, consider threading the food onto two of them. This prevents the food from rotating and better ensures an even cooking exposure.

- Threading zucchini and squash through their skin side gives the vegetables more stability on skewers.

- If your grilled ingredients will get mixed together (like in a grilled vegetable salad), chop 'em before you grill 'em and string like varieties on each skewer. Put 'em on the grill according to each veggie's required grilling time. (See Chapter 13.)

- To grill small stuff when a skewer won't do, use heavy duty aluminum foil. Punch a few holes in it so the smoke can get through to flavor the food it holds.

- So that they can handle the heat from the grill, soak combustible (wooden or bamboo, for example) skewers in water for at least a half hour to an hour before you intend to use them.

KABOB KOMBINATIONS

As you can tell by our title for Chapter 11, we believe that "variety is the *nice* of life." Nowhere is that more true than when it comes to creating kabobs. Here are some or our favorite combinations:

- Pieces of sausage add spicy appeal when threaded between other meats; they're especially good with chicken or lamb.

- Fresh sage leaves, prosciutto or bacon, and pork are delicious together.

- Try combining chunks of spicy Mexican or New Mexican sausage, chicken breast, and onion.

- Enjoy the contrast of a three-color fish kabob: salmon, tuna, and cod (or another white fish).

- Cubes of steak are wonderful when grilled beside shiitake mushrooms that have been marinated in olive oil.

- Shrimp in the shell marinated in olive oil, red pepper flakes, chopped garlic, and coarse salt is another favorite. Serve with wedges of lemon for squirting.

- Try polenta squares or triangles and portabello mushrooms. Brush them with a blend of garlic, olive oil and fresh thyme as they grill.

IF YOU'RE SO
INCLINED

Set out platters of the foods we've suggested in this section and let your family or guests build their own kabobs.

- Lamb chunks (first steeped in your favorite red wine marinade), onion, and sliced winter squash will soon become a family favorite, even among those who rebel at trying anything new. Serve it with chutney and a stack of warm flour tortillas or toasted French bread.

- Smoked chicken-apple sausage, red bell peppers, and asparagus go great together.

Don't discard those twig-gy stems when you cut back your herbs. Soak thyme or rosemary sprigs and use them as your skewers to impart additional flavor.

■ Thread together zucchini, small or half ears of corn, clams, New Mexican sausages, and fresh tuna and then marinate them in olive oil, lemon juice, a pinch of chili powder and cumin, and lots of garlic. Wonderful!

■ Try a selection of seafood, such as mussels, jumbo shrimp in the shell, squid, and crab. Brush them with a mixture of olive oil, garlic, and lemon juice as they grill. This combination is great when you serve it with a fruit salsa. (We provide the salsa recipes later in this chapter.)

■ For a new twist, try grilling vegetables and fruits together: eggplant, summer squash, bell peppers, sweet onions, cherry tomatoes, mushrooms, pine-apple, or peaches. Cut vegetables into $1/2$-inch slices or large chunks. Brush with warmed oil (seasoned with garlic or other herbs). Grill until tender. Turn only once. Fruit should be halved with pits removed. Grill as is (no oil needed), pulp side down. Or, thread a serving-sized combination onto each skewer.

If those suggestions haven't triggered some ideas of your own, not to worry. Go back and reread them and they soon will. The most important part of truly achiev-ing *The Lazy Way* to kabobs is to have fun while you cre-ate them.

FLEX THOSE FINGERS FOR THESE

In many ways, appetizers served outside at the picnic table, near the grill, serve the same purpose as those you present to your guests at a cocktail party or before dinner. It keeps them busy chewing and mingling. (We won't mention the occasional guest who sprays his food.)

While the function is the same, the foods you serve outside for this purpose are usually a little different. Not vastly so. But you do need to take into consideration such factors as food spoilage possibilities; therefore, don't leave any shrimp or egg dishes out in the sun for hours. Some dishes, such as the mushroom pate we're about to discuss, work well if you surround the serving bowl with chipped ice. You can grill stuffed mushrooms in shifts, so they come off of the heat at different times and don't sit around on the table for too long before the guests pop 'em in their mouths.

YOU'LL THANK YOURSELF LATER

Most appetizers can be prepared the night before. Your job is much easier if the mushrooms are already stuffed and you shape the meatballs ahead of time so that they're ready to pop on the grill 45 minutes to an hour before you need to serve them. Salsa is a dish that tastes better the next day.

Stuffed Mushroom Caps and Meatballs

We like to use the same meat to stuff mushroom caps and to create meatballs. That way, we don't have to worry about measuring precise amounts into each mushroom, so things come out even. We simply roll any leftover meat into meatballs and it looks like we planned the proportions we end up with. (It seems like there is always someone in a crowd who won't eat mushrooms. So, this variety serves two purposes.)

Servings vary

Button mushroom caps

Filling

1 Wash the mushrooms, pat dry, and remove the stems. (We reserve the stems to chop for mushroom pate—recipe given later in this chapter).

2 Stuff the mushroom caps with about a teaspoonful of your favorite flavored ground meat. Here are a few examples:

- Prepare the "Haggis, Haggis, The Clan's All Here" recipe from Chapter 17. (Pam likes to substitute ground pork and chopped beef heart for the lamb.) Use any leftover meat to shape into meatballs. Have dishes of barbecue or dipping sauce on the table to serve with this variety, such as the Peanutbuttery Pork Sauce recipe given below.

- Flavor 1¹/₂ pounds of lean ground sirloin or ground round with the ingredients called for in the Calypso Caribbean Steak from Chapter 8. Add oatmeal or cracker or breadcrumbs in $1/4$-cup increments until all liquid is absorbed. We love the flavor of this one as it is, but provide sauces or chutney for those who like adding that extra zing.

- Flavor $1^1/2$ to 2 pounds of lean ground sirloin or ground round with the marinade ingredients called for in the Pucker Up Grilled Steak from Chapter 8. Mix in $1/2$ cup of diced onion and a tablespoon of Worcestershire sauce. Add oatmeal or cracker or breadcrumbs in $1/4$-cup increments until all liquid is absorbed.

3 We sometimes wrap each and every mushroom individually in its own foil packet (for those times we put them on the back of the fire for the "chefs" to munch on during a long, slow-smoked meat grilling session). However, the most frequent way we grill these is by either placing the mushrooms cap-side down in buttered aluminum foil pie tins (to which we add a heavy-duty foil lid) or inside of foil packets. We put about a dozen meatballs in each foil packet; this works especially well if you need to stagger the grilling times. Place the packets on a medium grill for 45 minutes to an hour, depending on the size of the mushroom caps and the meatballs.

4 Remove the stuffed mushrooms and meatballs from the grill and set them out on serving platters surrounded by your choices of barbecue and dipping sauces. Provide holders containing toothpicks for those who wish to be dainty and not eat with their fingers. We usually place tongs beside the serving platters, too; this makes it easy for guests to transfer the meatballs and mushrooms to their plates.

QUICK ⬤ PAINLESS

For an easy yet delicious dipping sauce, add $1/2$ cup of jelly (we prefer red currant) to 1 cup of your favorite barbecue or chili sauce. This dipping sauce is especially good with grilled smoked sausage; since it's already precooked, all you do is heat it up, slice it, and provide toothpicks to stick in each slice.

Marvelous Mushroom Paté

Get those crackers, toast points, and celery sticks ready. You're gonna feel compelled to sample this one as soon as you make it. But go easy. You'll want to refrigerate the rest of it to serve your guests the next day; the flavors will be even better by then, anyhow.

Makes 3 cups

4 tablespoons butter

1 cup fresh mushrooms

$^1/_4$ cup shallots

$^1/_2$ cup chicken broth

One 8-ounce package of cream cheese

1 tablespoon scallions (white part)

Optional: fresh chives or scallion greens

1 In a grill-safe skillet, melt the butter and sauté the finely chopped mushrooms (we use the stems from the button mushrooms when we make stuffed mushrooms) and shallots until tender. Add the chicken broth and simmer until all of the broth is absorbed by the mushrooms and the liquid evaporates. Remove from the heat and transfer to a serving bowl.

2 Stir in the cream cheese and the finely chopped (non-sautéed) scallions. NOTE: If you prefer a stronger spread, substitute 2 minced cloves garlic and $^1/_4$ cup of finely-chopped scallion whites and greens for the shallots.

3 Chill until ready to serve. Garnish with finely chopped fresh chives or scallion greens, if desired.

QUICK n PAINLESS

If you find you don't have as many mushrooms as is called for in the recipe, make up the difference with some finely chopped grilled chicken breast. Or, in a pinch, adding some bread crumbs as filler is okay, as long as you don't use too much.

YO HO HO AND A BOTTLE OF TUMS

Yep! It's time to make salsa. It's simple, as you'll discover.

Minor's Base Salsa

Since our discovery of the Minor's bases (see Appendix A), not only do we dedicate shelf space in our refrigerators to these preservative-free timesavers, we've had a ball creating recipe variations as well. Here are a couple of our favorite salsa combinations.

Makes 1 cup

1 cup basic salsa mixture

$^1/_2$ teaspoon sautéed garlic base

$^1/_8$ teaspoon roasted onion base

$^1/_2$ teaspoon roasted red pepper base

Optional: $^1/_2$ teaspoon sun-dried tomato base

1   Add the bases to the cup of basic salsa and mix well.

Spicy Blend

$^1/_4$ teaspoon ranchero base

$^1/_4$ teaspoon ancho base

$^1/_4$ teaspoon chipotle base

1   Add all three ingredients to the base salsa.

YOU'LL THANK YOURSELF LATER

Don't limit your use of Minor's Base Salsa to tortilla chips; it makes a great veggie dip, too. It's also delicious as a topping for warmed-up leftover grilled chicken or beef, wrapped in a soft corn tortilla.

If you don't have time to plunge tomatoes into boiling water, remove the skins, and then chop your own, it's okay to use the kind that comes in a can. A 28-ounce can of diced tomatoes yields 3¹/₂ cups of tomatoes and juice. Enough for a lot of hungry appetites.

Build Your Own Salsa

Everyone's tastes are different. But, as you'll soon discover, it's easy to accommodate those idiosyncrasies by adding and subtracting a few ingredients. We usually start out making a salsa base. Then we divide it into 1-cup increments and adjust the seasoning. Let us show you what we mean.

Servings vary

Basic Salsa

Tomatoes and tomato juice

1 Dice tomatoes. To each 1 cup of diced tomatoes and juice, add:

1 tablespoon chopped shallot or

1 small chopped onion or

¹/₂ cup of chopped scallions

2 tablespoons fresh, chopped cilantro (or 2 teaspoons of freeze-dried flakes)

2 tablespoons lemon juice or

2 tablespoons lime juice or

1 tablespoon vinegar (the choice of what kind is yours)

¹/₄ cup virgin olive oil

2 Choose your ingredients and mix together in a glass bowl. Note: Lime juice is most often used in the spicier, traditional salsa.

3 Now it's time to add some variety. To each cup of salsa, add any or all of the following:

1 crushed clove garlic

$^1/_4$ cup chopped red or green pepper

$^1/_4$ cup drained, canned corn (or better yet, grilled fresh sweet corn, cut from the cob)

4 Depending on how hot you like your salsa, we recommend you start with $^1/_4$-teaspoon increments of the following and adjust accordingly:

Chili powder

Cayenne pepper

Red hot sauce

Jalapeño pepper, chopped

Ancho chili powder

Chipotle purée

5 Choose your seasonings and mix them in with the basic salsa.

YOU'LL THANK YOURSELF LATER

If you're watching your fat, you can eliminate the olive oil and create a fat-free salsa. Just remember to greatly reduce the amount of lemon or lime juice or vinegar, too. We recommend you start with only 1 teaspoon of juice or $^1/_2$ teaspoon of vinegar and adjust to taste.

Peanutbuttery Pork Sauce

As the recipe name suggests, this one is great with pork. (It makes a great basting sauce for grilled pork steak, too; just be careful because it will scorch easily.) We often make it the night before, in either the microwave or on the stovetop. It's your call. We give you the grilltop directions below. However you decide to make it, we're willing to bet you'll make it often!

Makes 1¹/₄ cup

1 tablespoon butter

1 small onion

2 cloves garlic

¹/₂ cup catsup

1 tablespoon Dijon mustard

1 tablespoon brown sugar

1 tablespoon honey

2 teaspoons paprika

1 tablespoon Worcestershire sauce

¹/₄ cup creamy peanut butter

2 tablespoons soy sauce

1 tablespoon white wine vinegar

1 In a grill-safe skillet, melt the butter over medium heat and then sauté the diced onion and chopped garlic until the onion is transparent.

2 Stir in the catsup, Dijon mustard, brown sugar, honey, paprika, and Worcestershire sauce, and continue to cook over a low heat for 10 to 20 minutes.

3 Remove from the heat and stir in the peanut butter, soy sauce, and vinegar. Serve warm or chilled.

Note: For those who prefer a spicier dipping sauce, stir in $1/2$ teaspoon of cayenne pepper and 2 teaspoons of ancho chili powder after you sauté the onion and garlic. Then, after you remove the sauce from the heat and add in the other ingredients, include a tablespoon of pureed canned chipotle.

IF YOU'RE SO
INCLINED

For a more robust sauce, add either powdered or chopped peppers (or those available from Minor's) like cayenne, ancho, and chipotle to your sauce.

FRUIT SALSAS

These chunky fruit sauces are a great complement to most grilled meats, poultry, seafood, or grilled and toasty cheesy tortillas (see recipe below). Our recipes are on the mild side. If you like your salsa hot, add your choice of chilies, black pepper, and cayenne pepper to the mix.

Peach Salsa

3 ripe peaches

1 tablespoon red onion

1 tablespoon lime juice

$1/8$ teaspoon salt

1 In a glass bowl, mix the peeled, pitted, and coarsely chopped peaches (or nectarines), chopped red onion, lime juice, and salt, stirring gently to combine.

2 Cover and refrigerate at least 1 hour to blend flavors. You can store this mixture in the refrigerator for up to 2 days.

YOU'LL THANK YOURSELF LATER

Most marinades should be mixed in glass bowls because the acidic ingredients can corrode some materials. We like to use glass dishes with clear glass lids; it's easier to do a visual inventory than trying to remember which color bowl we stored something in.

Plum Salsa

3 ripe plums

1 scallion

1 teaspoon freeze-dried basil leaves

1 tablespoon balsamic vinegar

Pinch salt

In a glass bowl, mix the pitted and coarsely chopped plums, chopped scallion (white part only), basil, balsamic vinegar, and salt, stirring gently to combine. Cover and refrigerate for at least 1 hour to blend flavors; this one may be kept in the refrigerator for up to 2 days.

Watermelon Salsa

1 cup watermelon

$^1/_8$ cup red onion

1 teaspoon freeze-dried cilantro

$^1/_2$ teaspoon honey

$^1/_4$ teaspoon cinnamon

1 teaspoon candied ginger root

1   In a glass bowl, combine the seeded and finely diced watermelon, minced red onion, cilantro, honey, and finely chopped candied ginger root, and toss lightly to mix.

2   Chill for an hour in the refrigerator to blend the flavors.

Note: If you don't have candied ginger and must use fresh, don't fret—just increase the amount of honey to taste.

QUICK 🐸 PAINLESS

Mix leftover fruit salsas together in a microwave-safe bowl. Cook on high 5 to 10 minutes, stirring after each minute, until juices evaporate and mixture thickens. You've just created what those of us with Pennsylvania Dutch heritage call a mincemeat-tasting sauce. Others call it chutney. It's great served alongside grilled meats, and it will keep up to a week in the refrigerator.

Always use a grill-safe pan—one on which all parts can withstand the high temperatures of the grill (no plastic or wooden handles, for example). Grilling supply stores carry them or you can use one made completely of cast iron.

Grilled Flour, Corn, or Cheesy Tortillas

Now that you have all of those great dipping sauces and salsas for your guests, you need something for them to do the dipping with. Sure, you could set out a couple of bags of packaged chips, but why? Especially when it's so easy to make these great variations. Again, get ready to build your own.

Servings vary

Garlic Oil

1/4 cup olive oil

2 cloves garlic

1   (a) In a grill-safe pan, sauté the minced garlic in the olive oil, strain, and set aside to use to brush onto the tortillas as you grill them. (See instructions below.)

Chili Butter

1 tablespoon olive oil

1/2 cup onion

1/4 teaspoon chili powder

1 tablespoon ancho chili powder

2 tablespoons lime juice

Salt

Freshly ground black pepper

1/2 pound butter

1 (b) In a grill-safe pan, heat the olive oil and then add the chopped onion and sauté it until transparent. Add the chili powders and continue to cook over low heat for 2 minutes. Remove from the heat and allow to cool slightly. Then add the lime juice and salt and pepper to taste and mix well. Add the butter and mix until well-blended.

2 Brush flour or corn tortilla shells with either the Garlic Oil or Chili Butter. Place oiled side down on the grill and brush the tortilla tops with the same mixture.

3 Grill until lightly browned and crisp, about 1 to 2 minutes per side, if over low to medium heat. Move to a platter or napkin-lined basket. Break the tortillas into serving-sized portions.

Cheesy Tortillas

1 Brush flour or corn tortillas with either the Garlic Oil or Chili Butter. Place oiled side down on the grill. Add grated cheese (such as cheddar, Swiss, mozzarella, or a combination of your favorites) to the center of each shell, being careful not to get the cheese too close to the edges of the tortillas; you don't want it to melt out of the shell and drip onto the coals and burn.

2 Place another tortilla atop of the grated cheese-topped tortilla. Brush the top of that shell with your choice of oil or butter. After about 1 to 2 minutes, or when the bottom shell is lightly browned, use tongs or a grill-safe spatula to turn the cheese-stuffed shells to grill the other side.

3 When the shells are lightly browned and the cheese is melted, transfer the shells to a serving platter and cut into wedges using a pizza cutter. Serve warm or slightly cooled with salsa or dipping sauce.

IF YOU'RE SO
INCLINED

Need a dipping sauce in a hurry? Add 1 tablespoon of Dijon mustard to $1/2$ cup of maple syrup. This one is great with Cheesy Tortillas.

Getting Time on Your Side

	The Old Way	The Lazy Way
Watching your wooden skewers go up in flames	5 minutes	0 minutes
Returning undergrilled food to the grill	5 to 10 minutes (because you failed to skewer like-sized pieces or ones with similar grilling times)	0 minutes
Failing to impress your guests with "fancy" barbecue or dipping sauces	30 minutes	0 minutes
Discarding herb stems	5 minutes	0 minutes
Being plum out of condiment ideas	30 minutes	0 minutes (you now have a plum salsa recipe)
Calling the haz-mat team each time the plastic handles on your pans ignite	5 minutes	0 minutes

Chapter fifteen

The Grilled Finale

Desserts! **Be they gooey and gloriously sticky or gummy and yummy or crunchy and punchy, for many of us, it's the conclusion of a meal that we crave. And best of all, there's no end to the sweet stuff you can fix on your grill.**

So, whether after a meal you want to relax over dessert, savoring a cup of coffee or a drink with friends or your significant other, or you need something tempting for later so you can bribe the kids to eat their veggies **NOW**, we're here to help. Forget about taking time to stop and smell the roses; that can trigger allergies. We believe in slowing down the pace long enough to enjoy the truly sweet things in life: desserts!

Everybody needs balance in his or her life. Sometimes some counterbalance is nice, too. And there's absolutely no need to feel guilty about scarfing down the sweet stuff. Instead, think of it as feeding your incentive to begin that exercise program.

Here are some suggestions to get you started.

If you have small children and you're tired of melted ice cream messes, then we have some good news for you. The chocolate mousse is firm enough that you can scoop it out like ice cream. So then, why put it in a bowl? Serve it in a cone instead.

Savory Same Ol' S'Mores

Everybody loves this scout and guide campout staple. They're easy. They're quick. They're delicious.

Makes 4 servings

2 milk chocolate bars (1.55 ounces each)

8 large marshmallows

4 whole graham crackers (8 squares)

1 Break each graham cracker and chocolate bar in half. Place half of a chocolate bar and 2 marshmallows between each of the two graham cracker squares. Wrap them in lightly buttered foil pieces.

2 Place on grill over medium-low grill for about 3 to 5 minutes or until chocolate and marshmallows are melted. (The grilling time will depend upon the grill temperature and whether it is open or covered.)

(Simpler Than Rice Krispy Treats) Chocolate Mousse

Let your guests and family think you slaved for hours making this dessert. You'll know better. But don't tell them how simple it is to make. The taste certainly won't give away your secret.

Makes 6 to 8 servings

One 8-ounce package of cream cheese

1 teaspoon vanilla

One 12-ounce package of semi-sweet chocolate chips

One 8-ounce container of frozen dessert topping

1 In a large bowl, mix together the cream cheese and vanilla.

2 The next step is to melt the chocolate. The process involves less risk of burning the chocolate if done in a grill-safe double boiler; however, as long as you watch it closely and stir it often, you can use a grill-safe pan or skillet placed over medium to low heat. Adding a tablespoon or so of milk to the pan or skillet will help make it easier to stir the melting chocolate chips to keep them from scorching. That small amount of liquid won't change the firmness of the mousse.

3 Pour the melted chocolate into the cream cheese and blend well.

4 Add the defrosted whipped topping and stir into the chocolate-cream cheese mixture until it's completely blended. Chill until ready to serve.

QUICK ⬛ PAINLESS

You don't necessarily need to heat up the grill to make the Chocolate Mousse recipe, especially if you plan to fix it the night before. You can either melt the chocolate chips in the microwave (on high, stirring it between 15- to 30-second nuking increments, being careful not to scorch the chocolate) or in a double boiler.

Who Goosed the Mousse?

For an adult dessert, we recommend substituting 4 tablespoons of liqueur for the vanilla. The following is how we make our favorite combination.

Makes 6 to 8 servings

One 8-ounce package of cream cheese

4 tablespoons (or more) coffee liqueur

One 12-ounce package of semi-sweet chocolate chips

One 8-ounce container of frozen dessert topping

1 In a large bowl, mix together the cream cheese and liqueur.

2 Follow steps 2 through 4 given for the (Simpler Than Rice Krispy Treats) Chocolate Mousse.

3 Spoon the mousse into a pastry bag and pipe it into sugar cones or your dessert dishes.

The Pie's the Limit

This is dessert that, with a little foresight, you can bake on your grill so it's ready to serve when you and your family or guests finish the main course.

1 spice cake mix

$1^1/2$ cups quick-cooking oatmeal

$^1/2$ cup butter

1 egg

$^1/2$ cup chopped nuts

$^1/2$ cup brown sugar

One 21-ounce can of apple or peach pie filling

Optional: $^1/2$ cup grated cheddar cheese

1 In a large bowl, combine the cake mix, 1 cup of the oatmeal, and 6 tablespoons of the butter. Mix until crumbly, reserving 1 cup of the resulting crumbs.

2 To the remaining crumbs, blend in the egg; if you intend to use apple pie filling, also add the $^1/2$ cup of grated cheddar cheese. Press this mixture into a buttered 12-inch pizza pan or 13×9-inch sheet pan. Grill for 12 to 15 minutes.

3 Remove pan from the grill and spread the pie filling over the crust.

4 In a small bowl, mix the remaining oatmeal, nuts, 2 tablespoons butter, and the brown sugar. Sprinkle this mixture over the top of the pie filling.

5 Return to the grill for another 15 to 20 minutes. Serve warm or chilled, cut into wedges or squares.

A COMPLETE WASTE OF TIME

The 3 Worst Things You Can Do with Hot Coals or Lava Rocks:

1. Douse them with water (you'll warp the grill and miss out on reasons 2 and 3).

2. Neglect to use the left-over heat to grill dessert.

3. Neglect to use the coals to make second helpings of dessert.

Stuck in a rut? Don't limit yourself to grilled fruit over ice cream. Grill angel food cake wedges over medium heat about 1 minute or until golden on both sides. For added flavor, brush with your favorite liqueur or some honey butter before you put the wedges on the grill.

Hot Fruit Salad

This will tempt you to heed that bumper sticker advice: Life's short; eat dessert first. Instead, save the best for last. A fantastic finale for a fine feast.

Makes 6 servings

1 medium pineapple

2 large bananas

3 medium plums

2 medium nectarines or peaches

$^1/_2$ cup honey

1 tablespoon fresh lemon juice

$^1/_4$ cup mint leaves or 2 drops peppermint oil

1   Cut the pineapple lengthwise into 6 wedges, leaving the leaves attached. Cut the bananas into thirds, the plums in half, and the nectarines or peaches into quarters.

2   In cup, stir together honey, lemon juice, and 1 tablespoon of the mint leaves or the 2 drops of peppermint oil.

3   With tongs, place all fruit pieces on grill over medium heat and grill for 10 to 15 minutes, turning the fruit occasionally until it's browned and tender. Brush fruit with some honey mixture during last 3 minutes of the grilling time.

4   To serve, arrange grilled fruit on large platter; drizzle with any remaining honey mixture. Garnish with fresh mint.

Bananarama RazzMaTazz

Don't worry about the alcohol content in this dish. The alcohol burns off when you ignite the sauce, so that after showmanship grilling worthy of the most demanding audience, all you're left with is marvelously flavored bananas and sauce to foster your favorite feeding frenzy fantasies.

Makes 8 servings

4 ripe bananas

4 tablespoons butter

2 tablespoons light brown sugar

$1/2$ teaspoon ground cinnamon

$1/4$ teaspoon ground nutmeg

$1/4$ cup banana or nut-flavored liqueur

$1/4$ cup light rum

1 Peel and slice the bananas.

2 In a large grill-safe frying or sauté pan, melt the butter over medium high heat. Add the bananas and slowly stir them while they heat and soften slightly. Add the brown sugar, cinnamon, and nutmeg, and stir for another 30 seconds.

3 Remove the pan from the flame, and add the liqueur and rum. Return the pan to the grill. The alcohol should now ignite. If it doesn't, you can ignite it with a match. Leave the pan on the grill until the flame burns off.

4 Serve the bananas and sauce over vanilla or praline ice cream, pound cake, or hot waffles.

QUICK 〈 📺 〉 PAINLESS

Grilling a ham and got some extra pineapple rings left over? Brush them with dark rum, grill a few minutes, turn the rings and brush with more dark rum. Sprinkle with brown sugar. Grill 6 to 8 minutes. Serve with scoop of ice cream or sorbet nestled in the center or dollop of yogurt.

To guarantee dessert is ready when *you're* ready to serve it, plan its grilling time so that it's done by the time you're ready to serve your meal. Then turn off the grill or set at its lowest temperature. Move dessert to a low temperature area to keep it warm.

Polka Dot Apples

Served plain or over ice cream or cake, your family will love this one.

Makes 4 servings

One 20-ounce can of apple pie filling
$1/4$ cup raisins
1 teaspoon lemon juice
2 tablespoons butter
$1/8$ cup packed brown sugar
$1/4$ cup oatmeal
Pinch salt
$1/8$ teaspoon ground cloves
$1/4$ teaspoon ground cinnamon

1 In a large bowl, mix the apple pie filling, raisins, and lemon juice together.

2 Ready an 18-inch square of heavy duty aluminum foil. Use 1 tablespoon of the butter to oil the "inside" portion of the foil that will be next to the food. Pour the apple pie filling mixture into the center of foil and spread it out a bit.

Note: If you prefer, you can butter an aluminum pie pan and use that instead. You can then just make your "lid" out of a single thickness of aluminum foil; use about a teaspoon of the butter to oil the inside of the foil lid.

3 In a small bowl combine the brown sugar, oatmeal, salt, ground cloves, and ground cinnamon. Mix well and sprinkle over the top of the apple pie filling mixture.

4 Melt remaining tablespoon of butter and drizzle it over the oatmeal mixture.

5 Bring the edges of the foil up and over the mixture, folding over the top to make a tent and crimping the ends by folding them over to seal the packet. (Or, if using an aluminum pie plate, cover the pie plate with a loose fitting piece of foil, butter side down, pinching the perimeter so it clings to the foil pan, but leaving some space against the top.)

6 Place packet over medium coals and grill for about 30 minutes. Serve warm.

QUICK ⬤ PAINLESS

Go ahead. Be adventurous. Experiment. Substitute $3/8$ cup of your favorite granola for the oatmeal, brown sugar, and spices in Polka Dot Apples.

Why make only one batch of rolls? Mix up a double batch of the crust recipe and turn half of it into rolls. Roll it up with your choice of ingredients inside and freeze the roll before slicing. Bring to room temperature and allow dough to rise a bit and grill or bake later.

Crust Isn't Just for Pizza Anymore
Rolls

The next time you make up a batch of "Pam's Breaking All of the Rules But It Works Pizza Crust" from Chapter 12, keep back some of the dough to use for breakfast or dessert rolls. We'll give you some suggestions, but these are only a guide. Use your imagination and create desserts of your own.

1 Roll out the section of dough as usual but rather than pre-grill the result, use it to create one of these:

- Generously butter the top of the crust and the sprinkle it with cinnamon, sugar, and some grated lemon rind. Drizzle on some vanilla. Add some chopped walnuts, if you like. Roll up and then slice, placing the rolls close together on a buttered pan. Drizzle maple syrup over the top of the rolls and grill for 15 to 20 minutes.

- Spread the dough with peanut butter and grape jelly or peanut butter and honey, roll, slice, place on a buttered pan, and grill for 15 to 20 minutes.

- Follow the steps in Option A, except substitute grated orange rind for the lemon and pecans for the walnuts.

Go wild! Come up with your own combinations.

THE VERSATILE DO-IT-YOURSELF DESSERT

Whether you need a dessert treat for the kids or the kid in you, one of these suggestions is sure to be just what the sweet tooth ordered. You see, s'mores isn't the only campout trick we know. Another favorite is what some people call:

Hobo Popcorn

Peanut or vegetable oil
Unpopped popcorn kernels

1 In the center of 18" x 18" square of heavy duty or a double thickness of foil, place one teaspoon of oil and one tablespoon of popcorn. Bring foil corners together to make a pouch. Seal the edges by folding, but be sure to allow room for the popcorn to pop. Tie each pouch to a long stick with a string. Give everyone a pouch and have them hold it over the hot coals, shaking constantly until all the corn has popped.

2 Season the popcorn with:

- Salt and butter
- Soy sauce and toasted sesame seeds
- Melted chocolate
- Melted peanut butter
- Melted caramels

Or season with your favorite flavored salt, be it a cheese, chili, or herb blend.

Congratulations! Because you now grill your dessert, you've saved yourself some time and you've found a way to keep the kids happy so you can relax for a while after your meal.

The Lazy Way

Getting Time on Your Side

	The Old Way	**The Lazy Way**
Running back and forth to check on the dessert in the oven	45 minutes	0 minutes
Cranking the air conditioner long enough to cool down the kitchen	15 minutes (doesn't include the time needed to cool all of that hot air you brought into the house with you each trip back and forth)	0 minutes
Yelling at the kids to settle down and let you enjoy your after-dinner cup of coffee	15 minutes	0 minutes
Time spent carefully guiding the kids into the house to get them into the tub to clean off sticky dessert residue	15 minutes	5 minutes (you're outside; now you just hose them down)
Thinking ripe bananas were only good in bread or muffins	30 minutes	0 minutes
Thinking pizza crust dough was only for pizza crusts	30 minutes	0 minutes

Chapter
sixteen

The Whole Shebang– Preparing Entire Meals on the Grill

There are very few indoor cooking methods that allow you to start a meal and then safely walk away from it. Sure, you can do that with a crock pot and, in some cases, with meals that you roast in the oven. But nothing lends itself to a haphazard, afterthought style of cooking like grilling does. With grilling, family activities can be your priority; the stuff cooking on the grill is secondary. In many cases, you can start your meal on the grill and only return to check on its progress when it's convenient for you.

Case in point: We have a friend who combines grilling, exercising, and entertaining her kids. Not an easy feat! But she has it down to a science. She starts her meal on the grill and then plans walks around the block, the number of which depend on the steps required to complete the meal. Families

as large as hers are rare these days. But, as you'll soon
see, she's figured out how to handle it.

Once she has the food on the grill, this mom then
begins a trip around the block. She leads her procession
pushing the baby in a stroller followed by the next child
on a tricycle, and the next one on a bike with training
wheels. The eldest is on foot, keeping the kids in line and
bringing up the rear in what looks like an unchoreo-
graphed version of the elephant's parade from Disney's
The Jungle Book or *Dumbo*.

It doesn't matter if you're able to get your spouse or
your teenagers to cooperate with that sort of plan
(which, in part, depends on whether or not one of them
will still fit in a stroller), you can still adapt your outdoor
cooking steps to accommodate your lifestyle—not the
other way around.

WE'LL SALAD IN THE SUNSHINE

The recipes in this section can serve as an entire meal.
We'll show you others in the "Side dishes NOT To Be
Pushed Aside" section that can accompany and comple-
ment an entrée.

It's Grilled Vegetable Salad Lime!

This salad's succulent fresh sweet corn, zucchini, yellow squash, and tomatoes acquire robust flavors from the citrus- and chili-infused dressing and smoky perfection from the grill. Serve this salad with the suggested lightly grilled cheese-and-onion-filled flour tortillas and you have a complete meal.

Makes 4 servings

Chili-Lime Dressing

$1/2$ cup extra virgin oil

3 tablespoons lime juice

$3/4$ teaspoon chili powder

$1/2$ teaspoon ground cumin

$1/2$ teaspoon salt

$1/4$ teaspoon garlic powder

Optional: 1 teaspoon sugar

Salad Fixings

4 small ears yellow corn

2 medium zucchini

2 medium yellow squash

4 small ripe plum tomatoes

4 green onions

Four 6-inch-diameter flour tortillas

8 tablespoons shredded sharp cheddar cheese

Lettuce leaves

1 Coat grill rack with nonstick vegetable cooking spray.

YOU'LL THANK YOURSELF LATER

You want food to stick to your ribs, not your grill rack. Therefore, don't just season the meal, season the rack, too. Herbs and spices go on the former; for the rack, either coat it with a generous amount of cooking oil or use nonstick vegetable cooking spray. We prefer the latter. It goes on fast sans mess.

QUICK PAINLESS

2 In a glass jar with tight-fitting lid, prepare the Chili-Lime Dressing by combining the oil, lime juice, chili powder, cumin, salt, and garlic powder until well mixed. Add the sugar, if desired. Set aside.

3 Carefully pull back husks from corn, leaving them attached at base, and remove all the silk. Lightly brush corn with some Chili-Lime Dressing. Place corn on tray while preparing other vegetables.

4 Use your discretion as to whether or not you first peel the zucchini and yellow squash. Cut them crosswise in half, then cut the halves lengthwise into $1/4$-inch-thick slices. Remove and discard the seeds. Place both varieties of squash on the tray with the corn. Brush slices on both sides with some dressing. Cut tomatoes lengthwise into halves and brush with some dressing.

5 Grill the corn over medium-hot coals until kernels are lightly browned, 8 to 10 minutes. Once it's done, transfer the corn to a tray.

6 Grill zucchini and yellow squash, turning occasionally until lightly browned, 2 to 3 minutes. Also transfer these to the tray once they are done.

7 Grill tomatoes, turning once, until just softened, which should take $1^{1}/2$ to 2 minutes. Transfer tomatoes to the tray with the other vegetables and set aside.

8 Finely chop the white portion of the green onion. Heat flour tortillas over low coals, turning often just until softened, 15 to 20 seconds. Sprinkle half of each tortilla with 2 tablespoons shredded cheese and one fourth of the chopped green onion. Fold tortillas in half and grill just until cheese softens. Fold tortillas in half again and transfer to tray with corn.

9 To serve, line 4 plates with some lettuce leaves. Cut corn kernels off cobs and set aside. Arrange one-fourth of zucchini and yellow squash alternately with each other on one side of each plate. Mound corn in center and garnish with tomato halves and folded tortillas.

10 Serve with the remaining Chili-Lime Dressing.

Substitute frozen corn, carrots, and green beans for the fresh vegetables. Toss the thawed vegetables with the dressing and evenly divide between four foil packets. Make pin holes in the packets so the veggies pick up smoke flavor. Place the packets on the rack over medium-hot coals; grill at least a half hour before you prepare your tortillas. Play "fetch" with your dog or look for four-leaf clovers with the time you save.

The Lazy Way

Cut the fat from your diet without cutting the taste. In most recipes you can substitute some chicken or other broth for some of the oil or butter and get the same great taste with a lot fewer calories.

Skewered Caesar-Style Chicken Salad

Many people assume that Caesar salad, a food fit for the gods, originated in Rome. Not so. It was actually created by a Tijuana chef, using what he had left on hand, to serve a large crowd of late diners. At the last minute, he threw in some bread crumbs…and the rest is history. We think you'll like our version, too.

Makes 4 servings

$^1/_2$ cup olive oil

4 cloves garlic

2 teaspoons dried rosemary

4 large boneless, skinless chicken breasts

32 1-inch cubes Italian bread

2 tablespoons lemon juice

1 teaspoon Worcestershire sauce

$^1/_4$ teaspoon dry mustard

$^1/_4$ teaspoon ground black pepper

Torn romaine lettuce leaves

$^1/_2$ cup green olives

$^1/_2$ cup black olives

4 tomatoes

4 tablespoons grated Parmesan cheese

1 Soak 8 bamboo skewers (to be used for the bread cubes) in water for a half hour.

2 In a small grill-safe saucepan, heat oil over medium heat and add minced garlic and cook 1 minute or until golden. Remove from heat and add the rosemary.

3 Rub the chicken breasts with $1/4$ of the seasoned oil and set aside for the 5 minutes it takes you to prepare the bread cubes.

4 Brush bread on all sides with about 1 tablespoon garlic-flavored oil and thread onto the bamboo skewers.

5 Place chicken breasts on the grill over medium-hot coals, grilling until done (15 to 18 minutes), turning once.

6 During the last few minutes of the chicken grilling time, place the skewered bread cubes on grill rack, turning frequently, until golden brown. Transfer bread to tray or plate.

7 Just before serving, stir the lemon juice, Worcestershire sauce, mustard, and pepper into remaining garlic-flavored oil; pour into small pitcher and set dressing aside. Ready 4 individual platters with $2^1/2$ cups of romaine on each. Divide the olives and chopped tomato between the salads. Top with 2 bread skewers.

8 Either place a chicken breast to the side of each salad or cut each breast into cubes and toss with the romaine.

9 Sprinkle each salad with 1 tablespoon of freshly grated Parmesan cheese.

10 Pass dressing to serve over salad.

QUICK ✦ PAINLESS

You can substitute purchased Caesar salad dressing for the garlic- and rosemary-flavored oil. Just be sure to get the regular dressing; while you can use the fat-free kind over your salad, it won't work as a coating for the chicken and bread.

Although fresh is best, to save yourself some time, pick up a bag or can of chopped walnuts. They are always available from the supermarket or, if you're lucky enough to live near one, from a local shelling plant.

Not Just Another Chicken Salad

The spinach makes this salad colorful. The sautéed walnuts add an extra dimension you must taste to believe! This salad will impress your friends and, best of all, it's easy to make!

Makes 4 servings

2 boneless, skinless chicken thighs

1 cup walnut pieces

1 tablespoon olive oil

$1/4$ teaspoon ground ginger

$1/2$ teaspoon candied ginger

4 tablespoons orange juice

2 tablespoons white wine vinegar

4 cups fresh spinach leaves

2 oranges or drained mandarin orange slices

1 cup sliced, fresh mushrooms

4 slices red onion

1 Place your grill wok or a grill-safe, heavy skillet over hot coals to preheat.

2 Cut the chicken into cubes and coarsely chop the walnuts.

3 Once the wok or skillet is warm, add the olive oil. When it starts to sizzle, add the chicken cubes and walnuts, stirring to coat them with the oil.

4 Sprinkle the ground ginger over the chicken and walnuts. Add the chopped candied ginger. Stir-fry until chicken is done, 5 to 10 minutes, depending on the temperature of your skillet.

5 Add 2 tablespoons of the orange juice to the skillet and continue to stir-fry until some of it is absorbed by the chicken. Remove the skillet from the heat and add remaining orange juice and white wine vinegar.

6 Tear the spinach into bite-sized pieces, then toss with orange sections, sliced fresh mushrooms, and red onion slices and divide among 4 plates.

7 Spoon the chicken mixture over the tops of the spinach salads and serve immediately.

A COMPLETE WASTE OF TIME

The 3 Worst Things to Do with Salads:

1. Limit yourself to complex salad preparations. Combine a mixture of chopped raw vegetables and chilled pasta and toss with your favorite dressing.

2. Forget to improvise. Substitute the woody stems from your thyme or rosemary plants for skewers for the Caesar-Style Chicken Salad. Read more about this in Chapter 14.

3. Fail to keep bags of frozen vegetables in your freezer. Most will work great in salads if you grill them until they're crisp tender, either inside a foil packet or stir-fried in your grill wok. (See Chapter 2, "Effortless Equipment Education.")

IF YOU'RE SO
INCLINED

Pumpkins aren't the only vegetables in the squash family that can serve extra duty. A stuffed acorn squash can act as its own container, too. And don't forget dual-duty fruit; nothing is more attractive than mixed fresh fruit served in a watermelon "bowl."

THE WORKS: CASSEROLE-STYLE AND MARVELOUS MAIN DISHES

During the summer, there's no reason to introduce even more heat into the kitchen by using your oven. Not when you have a grill. The recipes in this section show you what we mean.

Personal Pumpkin Casseroles

This recipe calls for canned vegetables. If you prefer to use fresh or frozen, you'll need to precook them a bit in order for them to get to the soup-tender consistency required of this dish. So that they experience the full hearty flavor of this dish, be sure to instruct your family or guests to use their spoons to scrape a portion of pumpkin into each bite.

Makes 4 servings

  4 pumpkins (small enough to sit on the grill rack with the lid closed, about 1 pound each)
  1 pound lean ground beef
  1 small onion
  $1/4$ teaspoon basil
  $1/4$ teaspoon thyme
  $1/4$ teaspoon rosemary
  $1/4$ teaspoon marjoram
  $1/4$ teaspoon cinnamon
  1 can creamed corn
  1 can whole kernel corn
  1 can French cut green beans
  2 tablespoons brown sugar

1 Cut out a lid on each pumpkin and remove the seeds and clean the inside.

2 Either in a grill-safe heavy skillet atop the grill rack or on your stovetop (if assembling the pumpkins in advance), brown the ground beef with the chopped onion, basil, thyme, rosemary, marjoram, and cinnamon until it is completely cooked. Drain the fat from the ground beef.

3 In a large bowl, mix the ground beef with the creamed corn and the drained whole kernel corn, drained green beans, and brown sugar.

4 Divide the mixture between the 4 pumpkins and put the pumpkin "lids" back in place.

5 "Bake" in a medium grill with the lid closed for 1 1/2 hours or until a toothpick can easily prick the flesh of the pumpkin.

6 Use pie plates as your individual serving dishes, so that if a spoon pierces the outside skin of the pumpkin, the juices will be contained. Garnish by placing the lid to the side in a dollop of sour cream.

QUICK ⚬ PAINLESS

Substitute fresh or frozen vegetables in this recipe. However, unless you like your veggies to be crisp, you'll need to pre-cook them so they can get to the soup-tender consistency we prefer for the Personal Pumpkin Casseroles.

Always keep some stand-by steaks in the freezer for those surprise visits by family, friends, or bosses. The time saved by not going to the market is worth it.

When You Don't Have Time to Be Impressive but Still Wanna Steak-and-Potatoes Meal

Yikes! Your spouse forgot to tell you that the boss and his or her spouse is coming for dinner: TONIGHT! You need something in a hurry, or preferably, faster. As long as you keep an emergency package of strip steaks in the freezer, you'll always be prepared. Seat everybody around the picnic table with a frosty-cold beverage in front of them (you'll find suggestions at the end of this chapter), light the grill, and within 10 minutes, you'll be ready to join them.

Makes 4 servings

Four 8-ounce strip or loin steaks

Lea & Perrins Worcestershire sauce

Balsamic vinegar

Garlic powder

4 baking potatoes, or 12 to 16 red potatoes

Salad fixings of your choice

1 Remove the steaks from the freezer, put them on a microwave-safe plate, and partially thaw them in the microwave. Note: Do not rush this step. If you use the high setting on your microwave, you'll partially cook the steaks and they'll be tough. Follow the manufacturer's directions for your specific machine. When in doubt, use the 50 percent setting for 3 minutes. You don't want them completely thawed because they'll set outside for about 10 minutes before you place them on the grill.

2 While the steaks thaw, select and wash the potatoes. Here are three suggestions on how to prepare them to impress your guests:

- Pierce each of the 4 large baking potatoes, put on a microwave-safe plate, and once you remove the steaks from the microwave, cook the potatoes on high for 5 to 8 minutes. Have 4 pieces of foil ready to use to wrap the potatoes once they're done in the microwave. We like to butter the portion of the foil that will wrap against the potato. Place a potato on each foil piece, then make an incision on the top of them into which you place a pat of butter. Wrap the foil around each potato.

- Once you've determined the number that will be sufficient for each serving, wash and pierce the small red potatoes. Follow the instructions in the bullet point above, only place 3 to 4 potatoes on each foil section.

- Clean and dice your choice of potatoes. Put them in a microwave-safe covered bowl and cook for 5 to 8 minutes, until just tender. (Be careful when you remove the lid so that you don't get burned by the steam.) Divide the potatoes equally and spoon them onto 4 buttered foil pieces that are large enough to wrap around the potatoes. Top with some butter and sprinkle with dill, or for an even better taste sensation, some chopped shallots. Shallots impart a flavor that we find is hands-down better than that which you get from onions or garlic!

3 While the potatoes are in the microwave, arrange your salad greens in individual bowls or, if you prefer to let your guests make their own, into paper towel-lined baskets. Most people don't mind assembling their own salads, so

QUICK ■ PAINLESS

Feel free to use the microwave to thaw your steaks if you're pressed for time. Just be sure to follow the manufacturer's suggestion regarding the time setting. Thawing a steak at a setting that's too high or doing so for too long can cause the meat to get tough.

simply grab a few bottles of salad dressing from the refrigerator to take with you to the picnic table.

4 Place the steaks on a platter to take them to the grill. Collect your dinnerware and napkins, the foil potato packets, the salad fixings, and the bottles of Worcestershire sauce, balsamic vinegar, garlic powder, and salad dressings, and you're ready to move outside.

At this point, unless you prefer to be a martyr, now is the time to yell for everyone outside to get up and help you do the carrying. (Be sure to make that request with a smile on your face so it reflects in your voice.)

5 Smile again, this time so they can see you do so, thank everyone for their help, and pour them some more of their beverages of choice to keep them occupied awhile longer.

6 Place the potato packets on the grill. You now have about 10 minutes in which to enjoy a little something cold to drink yourself.

7 Place the steaks on the grill rack directly over the medium-hot coals. Sprinkle each steak with generous amounts of the Lea & Perrins Worcestershire sauce, the balsamic vinegar, and some garlic powder. (We believe at this point flare-ups are our friend, for they allow us to sear the meat and seal in the juices.) You're not running a restaurant here, so it's up to you whether or not you wish to take "requests" as to how everyone would like their steaks. Even if those requests range from medium (the least done we'll prepare our steaks to ensure they've reached a temperature sufficient to destroy harmful bacteria) to well-well-done, by strategically moving the steaks to hotter and cooler portions of the grill, you can fix them so they all get done at the same time.

QUICK ▭ PAINLESS

A grouping of different types of salad greens, raw broccoli florets, and some baby carrots make an attractive presentation and, even better, makes it appear that you've worked harder than you have.

8 Once the steaks are ready to serve, instruct your guests and spouse (who should also be carrying your plate) to bring their plates to the grill. Slap a steak and a potato packet onto each plate, steer everyone back to the table, start fixing your own salad so they follow your lead, and now…after barely breaking a sweat…enjoy your meal!

Grilling season is year-round for both of us, despite the weather. The year-round part is easier for Keith; he's from Florida. Ohio native Pam has found that guests do complain when they have to take turns with the snow shovel to clean themselves a place at the picnic table, so she sometimes even lets them eat inside…if they promise to be neat about it.

YOU'LL THANK YOURSELF LATER

We follow the suggestions in Chapter 4 and keep a selection of condiments, salad dressings, and seasonings on a tray that we store inside the refrigerator in the garage. If you have the space for that luxury, it saves you the time of carting that stuff back and forth from inside of the house.

IF YOU'RE SO
INCLINED

Add small red potatoes to YooHoo Yogurt Chicken at the end of Step 3, before you cover the skillet. The amount of time you pre-cook the potatoes in the microwave will depend on their size and how long you plan to leave the skillet covered on the grill before you serve the meal.

YooHoo Yogurt Chicken

Give this one a chance! You'll be glad that you did. The blend of sweet onion and tart yogurt creates a sauce that pleases the palate without pouring on the calories. We sometimes like to double the amount of sauce called for in the recipe and add small red potatoes to the skillet before we add the chicken.

Makes 4 servings

8 boneless, skinless chicken thighs

1 tablespoon olive oil

2 cloves garlic

2 large yellow onions

2 cups plain, fat-free yogurt

Optional: 1 tablespoon chopped parsley

Optional: 2 teaspoons paprika

Optional: salt and pepper

1 Place the chicken over medium-hot coals and grill until juices run clear, 3 to 5 minutes on each side.

2 While the chicken is grilling, place a grill-safe heavy skillet (with a lid) over the hottest area of your coals to bring skillet up to temperature. Once it's hot, add the olive oil. When the olive oil sizzles, move the skillet to a cooler area of the grill and add the minced garlic cloves and onion slices. Sauté until onion is tender; do NOT brown.

3 Stir in the yogurt. If you're using the parsley, add it now. Use tongs to move the chicken from the grill and place it in the skillet with the yogurt sauce. Spoon some sauce over the chicken. (We like to push the onions to the side, add the chicken, and then spoon the onions over the chicken. This helps prevent the onions from browning during the remainder of the cooking process.)

4 Cover the skillet and leave on the grill for 15 to 30 minutes. To serve, move the chicken to a platter and pour the onion-yogurt sauce over the top. (Now is when you'll sprinkle on the paprika if you wish to use it and season to taste with the salt and pepper.)

Special note: Some brands of yogurt add gelatin as a thickener. This can cause the yogurt to separate during the cooking process. If this occurs, after you've removed the chicken to the platter, you can thicken the sauce by stirring in some cornstarch, arrowroot, or instant mashed potatoes, $1/4$ teaspoon at a time, until thickened. This dish is delicious even if you omit the "thickening" step, but the presentation is much more attractive (i.e., it looks nicer) if you take the time to do so.

QUICK ⬭ PAINLESS

Add some pizzazz to the Yoo Hoo Yogurt Chicken. Before you serve it, sprinkle on some paprika. The pretty red color provides an appealing contrast against the white "background" of the sauce.

Luau Luscious Pork Roast

This is another recipe that you can play with. Improvise to your heart's content. For example, when it comes to the sweetener, we prefer the robust full-bodied taste imparted by molasses; we offer alternative suggestions for those who prefer a milder flavor. Likewise regarding the amount of pineapple juice. The amount suggested in the recipe acts as a tenderizer. If you want your roast to have more of the pineapple flavor, double the amount of pineapple juice called for in the recipe. Fixing the roast gives you time to grill your potato and veggies at the same time.

Makes 4 to 6 servings

One 2-pound boneless pork loin roast

Marinade

1 small clove garlic

$1/8$ cup olive oil

$1/4$ cup unsweetened pineapple juice

$1/4$ cup sweetener (dark corn syrup, honey, molasses, or maple syrup)

1 tablespoon lime juice

1 tablespoon brown sugar

1 tablespoon Dijon mustard

$1^1/2$ teaspoon soy sauce

$1/2$ teaspoon coriander (cilantro)

$1/4$ teaspoon ground ginger

QUICK ⬭ PAINLESS

This marinade works great (and requires far less time to marinate) if you wish to use it on cheaper individual pork steaks; they'll taste anything but cheap if you do.

1 In a microwave-safe bowl large enough to hold the roast, sauté the chopped garlic in the olive oil by cooking on high for 15 to 30 seconds in the microwave.

2 Add the pineapple juice, sweetener, lime juice, brown sugar, Dijon mustard, soy sauce, coriander or cilantro, and ground ginger to the olive oil and garlic mixture. Reserve $1/4$ of this marinade to use to baste the meat during grilling; pour the reserved marinade into a covered jar and refrigerate until needed.

3 Place meat in the dish, turning to coat it with marinade. Cover the bowl with plastic wrap and refrigerate 8 to 24 hours, turning the meat occasionally to distribute the marinade.

4 Grill over medium coals for 1 to $1^1/2$ hours, or until a meat thermometer placed in the center of the thickest part of the meat registers 170°F.

YOU'LL THANK YOURSELF LATER

Luau Luscious Pork Roast is another recipe that can benefit from creative cooking. Omit the 1/4 teaspoon ground ginger and substitute 1/2 teaspoon (or more) of chopped candied ginger instead. You'll love the sweeter, subtle difference.

Salmonella is a major concern with chicken. Take every precaution to avoid cross contamination. The best way to ensure that chicken is done is to use a meat thermometer to verify when the white meat has reached 175°F (or 185°F if you check the dark meat).

Lemony Herb Roasted Chicken

Among our circle of friends, this recipe is known by an acronym created from the list of ingredients: MR. T Lemon Butt Chicken. Marjoram, Rosemary, Thyme, Lemon, Butt(er). Whatever you call it, we call it delicious.

Makes 2 to 4 servings

$^1/_4$ cup butter

$^1/_4$ teaspoon marjoram

$^1/_4$ teaspoon rosemary

$^1/_4$ teaspoon thyme

1 lemon

$2^1/_2$- to 3-pound whole chicken

1 In a grill-safe saucepan, melt butter and add the marjoram, rosemary, and thyme.

2 Make a small incision in the lemon and squeeze about a tablespoon of juice into the butter mixture. Then, pierce the lemon in several other places and put it inside the chicken cavity.

3 Brush half of the herb-butter mixture over the chicken and then place it breast side up on grill rack.

4 Grill for $1^1/_4$ to $1^3/_4$ hours uncovered until done, brushing the chicken with the butter mixture several more times. (If chicken browns too quickly, cover loosely with a "tent" made of aluminum foil.)

SIDE DISHES NOT TO BE PUSHED ASIDE

Nothing is easier to set in front of your family and friends than some dip and a selection of fresh veggies. Our simple "base" is delicious by itself—how you doctor it up is up to you. We offer some suggestions, but we're sure you'll come up with lots of other flavor blends on your own.

It's Not Yucky Yogurt Cheese Pasta Sauce

Try this for an unusual pasta accompaniment to your meal, especially those times you're serving a grilled entrée that you've basted with Italian dressing. We don't use any salt in this one. It's tart and strangely appetizing all by itself!

Per single serving

- 1 tablespoon shallots
- 1 tablespoon olive oil
- 2 tablespoons yogurt cheese
- 1 teaspoon mayonnaise
- *Optional:* Parmesan cheese

1 In a microwave-safe dish, sauté the chopped shallots in the olive oil. Stir in the yogurt cheese (that you made by draining fat-free plain yogurt in a coffee filter-lined, covered funnel placed so it could drain into a jar overnight). Mix in the mayonnaise.

2 Toss with cooked and cooled angel hair pasta. Sprinkle with freshly grated Parmesan cheese if you wish. Serve immediately.

QUICK ⬤ PAINLESS

When you know you'll be having guests the next day, consider taking the time the night before to make one of the chilled soups suggested in Chapter 17. That advance preparation will free up more of your time to spend with your friends.

When in doubt as to how you want to season your dip, do a trial run. Put a tablespoon of dip mixture in a small bowl and add a touch of whatever seasoning or base addition you're considering so you can sample the possibility before you mix up an entire batch.

Veggie Dip Base

1 cup fat free sour cream

1 cup real mayonnaise

Optional: 1 tablespoon lemon juice

1. Stir the sour cream and mayonnaise together in a small bowl. If you decide to use it, add the lemon juice now. (See the Quick 'n' Painless Sidebar with the Make-Ahead Magnificent Mint Lemonade Syrup recipe for a suggestion regarding the lemon juice.)

2. Use a full batch of the dip base recipe above to create a Green Goddess Dip by adding the pulp of one ripe avocado, 1/4 cup of chopped green onions, 1 teaspoon parsley, and salt to taste.

3. Doctor the dip by adding such ingredients as cream cheese, soy sauce, chopped onion, fresh or dried herbs, crisp bacon pieces, chopped tomato, or minced garlic. Some additions will require some time for the flavors to merge; others are ready to serve immediately.

See Appendix A, "How to Get Someone Else to Do It," for information on Minor's bases. Many of those are fantastic for creating unique dips. By adding a scant 1/4 teaspoon of each base per cup of dip, we've served such combinations as:

- sun-dried tomato and roasted red pepper dip
- herb-roasted onion (with a touch of the chicken broth base as a flavor enhancer)

- bacon and roasted onion

- roasted garlic

- fiery fiesta pepper dip from a combination of ranchero, chipotle, and ancho bases

**IF YOU'RE SO
INCLINED**

Start a new Thanksgiving tradition. Freeze extra Cucumber Slaw so you have some on hand for that holiday feast. Celebrations are always better when you can include something harvested from your (or at least from the guy who owns the produce stand's) garden.

Cucumber Slaw

Because this recipe will keep three months in the refrigerator, you can mix up a batch today and it'll be there ready to serve whenever you're ready to serve it. On those occasions when we've reaped an especially good harvest from the garden, we've divided a batch of this recipe into plastic containers and frozen some, too.

Makes 8 cups

6 or 7 cucumbers

2 green peppers

2 large sweet onions

2 cups sugar

1 cup white vinegar

2 tablespoons salt

1 tablespoon celery seed

1 Have a large bowl nearby to eventually hold all of the ingredients.

2 Wash, peel, and remove the seeds from enough cucumbers to yield 7 cups when they are sliced very thin. Do the same with the green peppers, which when chopped or sliced should equal a cup. (You can substitute more cucumbers instead of the green pepper if you prefer.)

3 Peel and chop the onions, which should also yield around a cup. Toss all ingredients together in the bowl and set aside.

4 Pour sugar and vinegar into a saucepan over a low heat, stirring until the mixture is warm enough to dissolve the sugar.

5   Add salt and celery seed to the vinegar mixture and stir.

6   Pour the warm vinegar mixture over the cucumbers, peppers, and onion and mix well. Transfer to glass jars and store in the refrigerator until served.

QUICK PAINLESS

With a little foresight, you can save yourself the "boiling the sugar and vinegar" step in this recipe. Don't throw out sweet pickle juice! Store it until you make Cucumber Slaw and use it instead!

IF YOU'RE SO
INCLINED

Toss some of the Sauer-kraut Salad together with chopped hard boiled eggs and grilled red potatoes for something different from the same ol', same ol' potato salad. Or, add the Sauerkraut Salad to a mix of sliced carrots, broccoli florets, and cauli-flower.

Sauerkraut Salad

Stop that! Don't wrinkle up your nose until you've tried this. You can substitute plain old cider vinegar for the sweet pickle vinegar (juice), but it won't be as good. Follow the recipe and you have a side dish that's good served alongside cottage cheese and even better if you use it in your Grilled Rueben sandwiches (lean corned beef, Swiss cheese, and sauerkraut on toasted rye bread).

$1^1/_4$ cup sugar

$^1/_4$ cup sweet pickle juice (or cider vinegar)

$^1/_4$ cup extra-virgin olive oil or vegetable oil

$^1/_4$ teaspoon salt

1 bag or large can of sauerkraut

1 cup celery

$^1/_2$ cup green pepper

$^1/_2$ cup sweet onion

1. In a large glass bowl, stir together the sugar, vinegar, oil, and salt until the sugar is dissolved.

2. Put sauerkraut in a colander and run cold water over it for a few minutes, until it is thoroughly rinsed. Use a spatula to press out the excess moisture, and then transfer the sauerkraut to the bowl with the vinegar mixture. Stir well.

3. Add the chopped celery, green pepper, and onion to the sauerkraut mixture and stir until well blended.

4. Store in the refrigerator in covered glass jars until ready to serve. Salad will keep several weeks in the refrigerator as long as the vinegar mixture covers all of the other ingredients. Add additional pickle juice if necessary.

Bravo Bacon "Baked" Onions

This versatile recipe makes a great side dish for steak or ham-burger sandwiches. Or use the bacon, add tomato, mayon-naise, and lettuce, and serve on thick slices of bread—toasted on the grill, of course!

Makes 4 servings

4 medium sweet onions

4 teaspoons butter

8 slices of bacon

1 Peel the onions. Cross-cut into the onions from the top two-thirds of the way down.

2 Divide a teaspoon of butter in between each of the 4 sec-tions you've created in each onion.

3 Measure out 4 pieces of foil large enough to generously wrap the onions, overlapping the foil at the top to seal. Lay out two pieces of bacon in the shape of an X across each piece of the foil and place onion in the center. Bring bacon up and over the sides of the onion to where it overlaps at the top. Wrap the foil up and over the sides of each onion, folding it over at the top to secure it.

4 Grill over medium coals for an hour, turning occasionally. (If you place the onion on a higher shelf in your grill and close the lid, it isn't necessary to turn the onion.) Keep in mind that if you're opening and closing the lid while you grill an entrée, the onions may take a bit longer to cook. Therefore, you may wish to start your onions and any other foil-wrapped vegetables 30 to 45 minutes before you're ready to grill your entrée, then move them to the higher rack for the remaining 15 to 30 minutes.

YOU'LL THANK YOURSELF LATER

Remember, each time you open the lid you can add up to another 15 minutes to the grilling time. Only lift the lid when you have to, such as to turn the entrée. The food'll be fine. You're a grill chef, not a babysitter.

NOW FOR SOMETHING TO GO DOWN COOL AND EASY

Man does not live by canned soft drinks and fermented beverages alone. Sometimes it's nice to break out of a rut and try something different. For those times you're ready to do just that, may we suggest the beverage recipes that follow.

Energy Booster Punch

Years ago we heard a "home remedies" doctor on a radio talk show claim that this fruit juice mixture could boost your energy, especially if you add a teaspoon of cider vinegar to each glass. We skip the vinegar part; however, we do often use seltzer water in place of plain water to create a fizzy thirst quencher. This is one way to give your family a healthy soft drink substitute.

1 can frozen apple juice concentrate
1 can frozen pineapple juice concentrate
1 can frozen grape juice concentrate
1 can frozen cranberry juice concentrate
Water per instructions on the cans

1 Mix all juice concentrates together. We prefer to store the concentrate mixture in a covered container (a 2-liter empty seltzer bottle, for example), add the appropriate amount to a pitcher or individual glasses, and mix in the water when we're ready to serve it. If you wish, you can add the water per the instructions on the cans immediately. Store in your refrigerator. Serve chilled.

QUICK ☜☞ PAINLESS

Instead of ice for those cool drinks, use frozen melon balls or other frozen fruit. Make and freeze your own melon balls or pick up a couple of bags of 'em from the freezer case at your local supermarket. The added flavor from strawberries or melon balls will give a boost to sweet iced tea or any citrus soda.

Innocent Margaritas

As you'll see by the recipe that follows this one, we don't like getting stuck in a standard lemonade rut, either. Variety is also the thirst quencher of life.

8 large limes

1 large Valencia orange

3/4 cup sugar

6 cups water

1 Wash the limes and the orange, then slice them in half and squeeze their juices into a pitcher. Place lime and orange hulls into the pitcher, too.

2 Stir in sugar. Use a wooden or heavy plastic spoon to crush lime and orange hulls with juice and sugar to release the citrus oil.

3 Add water to mixture and stir well.

4 When you're ready to serve, in a blender add 1 cup of ice to every 1/2 cup of lime/orange mixture. Blend well until you have a frosty, slushy drink. Pour into chilled margarita glasses and garnish with a lime slice, if you wish.

Whether you make it with the mint or omit that step, we've found that substituting a tablespoon of Make-Ahead Magnificent Mint Lemonade Syrup for the lemon juice adds a delicious dimension to any dip.

Make-Ahead Magnificent Mint Lemonade Syrup

According to our experience, you usually get around 1 cup lemon juice from 4 medium to large lemons. Keep that in mind when you're planning the amount of syrup you wish to prepare.

$2^1/_2$ cups water

2 cups sugar

1 cup fresh lemon juice

$^1/_2$ cup fresh orange juice

$^3/_4$ cup mint leaves, loosely packed

Optional: mint sprigs for garnish

Optional: thin lemon slices for garnish

1 Pour water and sugar into a grill-safe saucepan over medium heat. Stir until the sugar dissolves and then allow the mixture to simmer for 5 minutes. Remove from the heat and let the mixture cool while you ready the other ingredients.

2 Cut fruit in half and extract juice. Add the lemon and orange juices to the sugar syrup.

3 Rinse mint leaves and pat dry. Put the mint leaves in the bottom of a 4-cup glass measuring cup. Pour sugar syrup over the mint leaves and let stand for an hour. Strain resulting syrup into a jar. (This lemonade base can be stored covered for several days in the refrigerator.)

4 To serve: Mix $^1/_3$ cup of lemonade syrup in a glass with $^2/_3$ cup water or seltzer water. Fill the glass with ice cubes. Garnish with a mint sprig and a lemon slice, if desired.

Good Golly Good Ginger Ale Syrup

Here's one way to know the formula for your soft drink. It's up to you whether or not you divulge it to your friends.

Makes 4 servings

   1 cup water

   1 or 2 ginger roots

   1 cup cane sugar

   1 tablespoon vanilla

   4 cups seltzer water

1   In a grill-safe pan over the hottest portion of the grill, bring water to a boil. Peel and slice enough ginger to fill 1 cup and move the pan to an upper rack or cooler area. Allow mixture to simmer for a half hour.

2   Remove the pan from the heat, and with a slotted spoon remove the ginger. (Optional: Strain the ginger water through cheesecloth to remove any ginger pulp.)

3   Add the sugar and stir until it dissolves. If necessary, return the pan to the heat long enough so no sugar crystals remain.

4   Add the vanilla.

5   For each serving, put $1/4$ cup of the resulting ginger ale syrup into a glass—over ice, if you wish. Pour in 1 cup of chilled seltzer water. This will mix with the syrup and cause a "head" to form on the drink. Store any leftover syrup in a covered glass jar in the refrigerator for up to a week.

YOU'LL THANK YOURSELF LATER

Whenever you make Good Golly Good Ginger Ale Syrup, remember the "ginger" bite can vary—sometimes one ginger root is stronger than another. Try a test sample, mixing 1 tablespoon of syrup to 4 tablespoons of water. That way you'll know if you find the drink too strong or too sweet and can adjust the amount of seltzer water accordingly.

There! This chapter should give you plenty of ideas about using your grill to help you prepare entire meals. But wait! That's not all! There's still Chapter 17, which includes soup, breakfast, sandwich, and packet meal recipes. And we haven't forgotten about your sweet tooth. Turn back to Chapter 15 for lots of dessert ideas, many of which you can leave unattended to "bake" on your grill while you enjoy your meal with the rest of your friends and family.

IF YOU'RE SO
INCLINED

For a delicious citrusy drink, add a cup of lemon-ade, limeade, or orange juice to each serving of ginger ale made with our Good Golly Good Syrup recipe.

Getting Time on Your Side

	The Old Way	The Lazy Way
Only grilling hamburgers and hot dogs	15 minutes	0 minutes
Cooking a meal instead of spending time on a family recreational activity	60 minutes	15 minutes
Wondering what the elephant parades look like in Disney's *The Jungle Book* and *Dumbo*	60 minutes	0 minutes (you've found time to watch the videos with your family)
Tending the oven while your family relaxes outside	60 minutes	0 minutes
Wondering what artificial colors are in the carbonated soft drinks you serve	60 minutes	0 minutes (you make your own syrup and use seltzer water)
Whistling "Dixie"	60 minutes (while you tend the meal)	60 minutes (except you're not just whistling "Dixie"—you're enjoying walks around the block and other leisure activities, too)

All Kinds of Other Stuff

As you can probably tell, we're firm believers that slaving away in the kitchen is a poor excuse for missing a sunrise, noonday sun, dusk, or a sunset.

This chapter contains around-the-clock suggestions for breakfast, a grilled sandwich, cold soups, packet meals, and the occasional midnight eclipse snack, too.

QUICK **n** PAINLESS

Scrapple served with some eggs, hash browns, and fresh fruit makes a wonderful meal.

Scrapple

Unlike the original Pennsylvania Dutch version of this recipe that uses pork parts we don't like to think about, this one is not only quick and easy, it uses sausage.

Makes 8 servings

1 pound sausage

One 12-ounce can of evaporated milk

$3/4$ cup cornmeal

1 teaspoon sugar

1 Over medium heat, fry the sausage in a grill-safe skillet until meat is completely cooked. Use a spatula to turn the meat often so it doesn't get too brown and to break it into the smallest pieces possible.

2 Add the evaporated milk and heat to the boiling point. Add the cornmeal and sugar and continue to cook, stirring often, for about 5 minutes or until the mixture thickens.

3 You can serve it directly from the pan in mush form. Or, if you wish to make it ahead, you can pack it in a loaf pan and chill it for later; then, cut it into 1-inch-thick slabs, coat it in some cornmeal, and fry it up in butter.

Slumgolly

Fix this for breakfast or brunch and you'll never look at scrambled eggs the same again.

Makes 8 servings

1 pound bacon

1 large yellow sweet onion

4 large potatoes

8 eggs

$^1/_4$ cup milk

16 slices of bread

Salt and pepper to taste

1 Cut the bacon into bite-sized pieces and fry over medium heat in a large grill-safe skillet.

2 While the bacon is frying, peel and dice the onion and potatoes. Drain most of the fat from the bacon and discard. Add the potatoes to the skillet and grill with the pan covered for 5 to 10 minutes, stirring and turning the potatoes several times during the process, until the potatoes are tender. Add the onion and sauté until they are clear.

3 Crack eggs into a large bowl and whip them together with the milk. Tear the bread into bite-sized pieces and toss in the egg mixture. Pour the egg and bread into skillet and toss with the bacon, onion, and potatoes until well mixed.

4 Continue to fry uncovered on the grill until the eggs are set, 8 to 10 minutes. Use a flat-edged metal or heavy plastic spatula to turn the mixture often, scraping the bottom of the skillet as you do so to ensure the mixture is not sticking. Be sure to switch to a different utensil to use to stir the eggs during the last few minutes of frying time to avoid salmonella contamination.

IF YOU'RE SO INCLINED

If you'd like to add some color and an added flavor boost to the Slumgolly, toss in a half cup of diced green and red peppers and sauté them with the onion.

PACKET MEALS, OR YOU DON'T ALWAYS HAVE TO FRY IT UP IN A PAN

There's no limit to the number of dishes you can create on the grill using the packet method. Keep in mind that the foil dimensions given throughout these recipes are intended as a guide only. As always, feel free to put your "fingerprints" on our suggestions and alter them to make them your own creations; simply adjust the size of the aluminum foil section as needed. See Chapter 3 for additional information on how to create a packet.

Build a Better Bird's Nest

This one takes a little bit more preparation time (unless you sneak in frozen hash browns in place of the freshly-grated potato), but once it's on the grill, you can forget about it until it's done.

Per serving

2 slices of bacon

1 large potato

1 egg

Optional: grated onion

Optional: diced green and red pepper

Optional: salt and pepper

1   In the center of an 18×18-inch square of heavy duty aluminum foil, criss-cross the two pieces of bacon.

2 Clean (and peel, if you prefer) and grate the potato. Mix in the onion, peppers, and seasoning, if used, then shape it into a ball.

3 Place the potato ball in the center of the bacon cross. Press it down so it forms a base that rests on the bacon, then take your thumb and create a nest in the center of the hash browns.

4 Crack an egg into that nest. Pull the resulting 4 ends of the bacon up and over the nest; then do the same with the foil, folding it into a packet that retains the shape of the nest.

5 Grill over medium heat for 30 to 45 minutes. Open the packet, being careful not to get burned by the steam that will escape. The nest is done if the bacon and potatoes are crisp on the outside and the egg is firm. If you wish to "crisp" it a bit more, return the packet to the grill with the top left open for another 5 to 15 minutes.

A COMPLETE WASTE OF TIME

The 3 Worst Things to Do With a Packet Meal:

1. Only use pizza crusts (see Chapter 12) for pizza. Toasted over the grill, they make excellent flatbread to serve with packet meals.

2. Only keep pizza sauce on hand for pizza. Use it in a pizzaburger-lasagna-style packet meal made of sliced potatoes, ground beef, pepperoni, mushrooms, cheese, and pizza sauce. Use a layer of the meat mixed with pizza sauce for the top and bottom layers to help prevent the meal from sticking to the foil.

3. Think that the only way to fix a pizzaburger-lasagna-style packet meal is with potatoes. Try it with other vegetables too.

Haggis, Haggis, The Clan's All Here

While he still might don his kilt durin' the grillin', Keith's otherwise Americanized this recipe. Just don't let him hear you say "glorified meatloaf." Smile and tell him it's "authentic tastin'" and everyone's life will be easier.

Makes 8 servings

1 pound boneless ground lamb

$1/2$ pound lamb liver

$1/2$ cup beef broth

1 small onion

1 large egg

$3/4$ teaspoon salt

$3/4$ teaspoon black pepper

$1/2$ teaspoon sugar

$1/4$ teaspoon ground ginger

$1/8$ teaspoon ground cloves

$1/8$ teaspoon ground nutmeg

1 cup old fashioned oatmeal

4 large potatoes

8 carrots

1   In a large bowl, mix together the ground lamb, liver cut into cubes, diced onion, and all of the other ingredients, except for the potatoes and carrots. Don't worry about getting it completely mixed at this point, because as you'll soon discover, you're about to get your hands dirty anyhow, so you might as well finish mixing it then.

2 Clean and slice the potatoes and carrots. Ready eight 12-inch or larger squares of heavy duty aluminum foil by first spreading them across your counter. (You're gonna get your hands dirty here in a minute, remember? This will save you from having to wash your hands between steps, so stick with us on this!)

3 Grease a 6-inch circle in the center of each piece of foil. Layer the potato slices from half of one potato and one sliced carrot in the center of each circle.

4 Now return to that waiting bowl of haggis mix. Squeeze the meat between your fingers. Move it around in the bowl. You want to make sure it's completely mixed and that the oatmeal has absorbed the broth by this point.

5 Next, one by one shape $1/8$ of the haggis mixture into a hamburger-sized patty portion and set it atop the potatoes and carrots. Once you've made all 8 haggis patties, you're excused for a minute to go wash your hands.

6 Seal each foil packet by folding over the edges. You'll turn these packets several times while they're on the grill, so you want to be certain they're well-sealed so that the potatoes and carrots benefit from the steam from the meat juices. We often place another piece of foil across the seam-side (top) of the packet and then turn it over and fold the foil over on the other side; this ensures that it's well-sealed.

7 Place each packet over medium coals and grill for 45 minutes to an hour, or until carrots and potatoes are tender. Turn the packets every 10 to 15 minutes. Keep the grill lid closed between turns.

IF YOU'RE SO
INCLINED

You can *Americanize* the haggis recipe some more and substitute ground beef and beef liver for the lamb.

Squash That Pork Chop, Honey

This is a meal you can prepare the night before and prebake it for 45 minutes in a 400°F oven, if you wish. Take the packets directly from the refrigerator and place on the grill rack over medium coals. They will be ready in about 30 minutes. Otherwise, follow the instructions given below.

Makes 2 servings

Two 1-inch-thick pork chops
1 acorn squash
2 tablespoons brown sugar
2 tablespoons honey
2 tablespoons butter

1 Place each pork chop on an 18×12-inch section of heavy duty aluminum foil. Season to taste.

2 Cut the acorn squash in half and remove the seeds.

3 Place each squash half on a pork chop, cut side up. Fill the hollow of each squash with 1 tablespoon each of the brown sugar, honey, and butter.

4 Bring the foil up and over the pork chop and squash half to form a packet, folding it to secure it.

5 Grill for an hour over medium coals.

Toasted Ham Sandwiches

Dijon mustard goes through a subtle flavor change when slowly heated in this manner. You have to taste these to appreciate what that difference does for a ham sandwich.

Per serving

1 deli-style hamburger bun

1 slice baby (mild) Swiss cheese

One $1/4$-inch slice of ham

$1/2$ teaspoon Dijon mustard

$1/2$ teaspoon butter

1 Spread $1/4$ teaspoon of the Dijon mustard on the inside half of each bun. Place the cheese and ham on the bun to form the sandwich.

2 Spread $1/4$ teaspoon of the butter on the outside of both halves of the bun. Place the sandwich in the center of a 6×12-inch piece of heavy duty aluminum foil. Bring the foil up and over the sandwich, folding it to close it and form a packet.

3 Grill over low heat for 15 to 30 minutes.

IF YOU'RE SO
INCLINED

You can make Toasted Reuben Sandwiches using this method, too. Use rye buns, Thousand Island dressing, some sauerkraut, corned beef, and Swiss cheese. Or change the pace (and the taste) of your Toasted Ham Sandwiches by using rye buns and adding some coleslaw to them before you wrap 'em in foil.

Use a soup base (see Appendix A) to make broth. In most cases, you simply dissolve 1 teaspoon of base into each cup of water. If a recipe calls for a bouillon cube, use 3/4 teaspoon of a base in place of each cube. Soup bases are much lower in sodium than are bouillon cubes.

SLURPS ON

Soup and a sandwich can make a meal. Here are three suggestions for cold soups you can prepare ahead of time. See the instructions with each recipe for information on how long you can store these soups in the refrigerator.

Ruby Doobie-Do

This recipe calls for tomato juice, but we think it's just as good if you use a tomato-vegetable juice, such as V-8, instead. This one is good hot or cold. It can be kept in the refrigerator for 4 days.

Per serving

$^1/_3$ cup beef broth

$^1/_3$ cup tomato juice

$^1/_3$ cup water

1 Stir the ingredients together in a coffee mug. Place the mug in the microwave on high for 30 to 60 seconds if you prefer a warm soup. Otherwise, serve immediately.

2 If you wish to store the soup in the refrigerator, do so in a covered jar.

A Cucumber Number

This soup is meant to be savored cold. Its subtle green color looks great when you serve it up in a crystal mug. It'll keep for 48 hours in the refrigerator. Just remove the covered jar of soup and shake it up to blend any ingredients that may have separated or settled, pour it into a mug, and serve.

Makes 4 servings

2 medium cucumbers

$1^1/2$ cups buttermilk

1 teaspoon salt

$^1/8$ teaspoon pepper

1 teaspoon dried minced onion

1 Clean (and peel if the skin is tough) the cucumbers. Cut into quarters and remove seeds, then puree in a blender or food processor along with $^1/4$ cup of the buttermilk and the dried minced onion.

2 Add the salt, pepper, and remaining buttermilk and process until well-blended.

3 Chill in a covered container until ready to serve. (It's best to chill this soup for at least 2 hours before serving so the flavors can meld.)

Congratulations! Serving cold soup adds pizzazz to your grilled dinner and making it is so quick and easy. The best of both worlds!

The Lazy Way

IF YOU'RE SO
INCLINED

Not Your Grandma's Chicken Soup is also great if you substitute milk for half of the water and vichyssoise it up a bit; that version is made even better if you float some half and half on the top of each serving and sprinkle on some snipped fresh chives.

Not Your Grandma's Chicken Soup

Okay, we're gonna cheat a bit with this one and use instant mashed potatoes. Of course, you're welcome to boil and puree the equivalent amount of fresh ones if you wish. This one is another soup with some versatility. It's delicious hot or cold if you serve it as stated in the recipe. It'll keep for 3 days in the refrigerator, so we're giving you instructions on how to make a big batch.

 1 small onion
 2^1/$_2$ cups chicken broth
 1^1/$_4$ cups instant mashed potato mix

1   In a grill-safe saucepan over medium coals, grate the onion and add it to 1 cup of the broth.

2   Heat the mixture until it boils, reduce the heat (or move to a cooler spot on the grill) and simmer covered for 10 minutes.

3   Remove from the heat and add the instant mashed potatoes; beat with a fork until the potatoes are fluffy.

4 Stir in the remaining broth and heat until the mixture once again comes to a boil.

5 Remove from the heat and serve; or cover and chill for later.

QUICK ☎ PAINLESS

Making soup "from scratch" doesn't mean you can't use shortcuts. When we need a cup of broth, we add a teaspoon of soup base to a cup of boiling water. If the recipe tells us to reduce that broth, we simply reduce the appropriate amount of water.

Midnight at the Oh Taste Us

Now for those promised late night snacks. This is another build-your-own-flavor recipe. We'll give you some suggestions. Once you get the hang of it, you'll then want to create your own. This recipe provides a great way to keep the kids busy outside (yet close enough you can keep an eye on them) when the inevitable munchies strike during your child's sleepover or slumber(less) party.

Servings will vary

Basic ingredients

Graham crackers

Butter

Sweetened condensed milk

Suggested ingredients:

Coconut

Caramels

Pecans

Chocolate chips or kisses

Bananas

Marshmallows

Peanut Butter

Jelly

1 If you're letting the kids assemble their own, you'll need a piece of foil for each dessert. We recommend creating a packet, but that's optional. You can place all of the snacks on a grill-safe tray if you prefer; if you do, we recommend you line it with foil, as these are messy.

2 Butter each side of a graham cracker. (This creates the crust.) Drizzle some sweetened condensed milk over the top of the graham cracker and then top it with your choice of ingredients, some suggestions of which are:

- pecans, caramels, chocolate chips
- peanut butter, banana slices, another layer of sweetened condensed milk, chocolate chips
- peanut butter, jelly, marshmallows
- pecans, caramels, chocolate chips, coconut, marshmallows

3 Grill for 5 to 10 minutes, using an indirect and low heat method, until the chocolate is melted and the sweetened condensed milk bubbles. Watch these carefully because the graham cracker will burn.

4 The individual foil packets can serve as serving plates. Otherwise, if you prepared these on a grill-safe tray, use a spatula to lift each snack and serve it on a paper plate. (Now take a break while the crowd enjoys their treats, but be ready to hose off a bunch of sticky kids when they're done eating.)

YOU'LL THANK YOURSELF LATER

You can create a temporary additional grill shelf by placing two bricks on your existing rack and topping them with another grid. This raises the rack even further above the fire, so it works especially well for foods that tend to scorch easily.

Getting Time on Your Side

	The Old Way	The Lazy Way
Missing out on a sunrise	15 minutes	0 minutes
Missing out on the noonday sun	60 minutes	0 minutes
Missing out on a chance to enjoy the afternoon sun	240 minutes	0 minutes
Missing out on dusk	15 minutes	0 minutes
Missing out on the sunset	15 minutes	0 minutes
Missing out on life	Far too many minutes	0 minutes

More Lazy Stuff

How to Get Someone Else to Do It

Bet you were expecting instructions on how to put your feet up, how to delegate all of the parts of the work you don't like to do, and where to get the negotiating skills necessary to make those receiving the orders happy to comply with your wishes, weren't you? (We're still researching that subject. But, we promise, once we figure that part out, we'll write and let you know about it.)

So, although not as easy as looking through the Yellow Pages to find a caterer and a cleaning service, we can offer you some tips to get others to do things for you *The Lazy Way* that are a bit easier on the budget.

As for the cleaning part, following the suggestions we make in Chapter 5 will help you out there.

If, on the other hand, you'd like some suggestions that will make your grilling chores easier, read on. While we can't list every solution in this small space, we do give you the names of some companies to get you started on your efficiency adventure.

BASES AND OTHER FOOD PRODUCTS

Since our discovery of bases—those highly concentrated broth, seasoning, and sauce mixtures that, unlike gritty bouillon cubes, are low in sodium and free of preservatives and (in most cases) MSG—we've become almost evangelical about spreading the word about them. We just can't say enough good things about bases; they truly deserve a place in every *Lazy Way* kitchen. Bases that can sit on your pantry shelf are much higher in sodium and often contain preservatives which we believe alters the flavor (and not in a good way), so we prefer the kind that require refrigeration. Those brands (Minor's and Redi-Base) are difficult to find in most stores. Many restaurant supply outlets carry them, as do some specialty stores. To ease your search, we're including company name, address, phone number, and Web site information on the two brands we use.

Sure, we sometimes still make our own chicken and beef broth and freeze it up in ice cube trays (later transferring those $\frac{1}{8}$-cup cubes to freezer bags). But we also dedicate a refrigerator shelf to bases!

If ease of use isn't enough to convince you to try bases in your own grilling recipes, how about this—they're also economical. Our budgets aren't that much different than those of most fireside chefs. We simply don't have the funds to purchase lobster and other fine seafood and boil it down to make broth. We let Minor's and Redi-Base do that for us! Read on to learn how you can, too.

If You Need the Broth, Minor's Has the Base

ALLSERV, Inc.
P.O. Box 21743
Cleveland, OH 44121
Phone: (800) TASTE-2-U (827-8328)
Fax: (216) 381-7170
E-mail: cooking@allserv.com
Web site: http://allserv.com/
Complete product list: http://allserv.com/quikorde.htm

Distributed exclusively by ALLSERV, Inc., Minor's bases include vegetable, chicken, beef, pork, ham, bacon, veal, turkey, clam, crab, fish, lobster, seafood, shrimp, sautéed garlic, and mushroom—most of which are also available in reduced sodium, low-salt varieties.

Special sauce preparations include sun-dried tomato, Alfredo, white wine cream, demi glace, hollandaise, and a red sauce. Signature™ Flavor Concentrates include roasted mirepoix (a delicious medley of fire-roasted carrots, onions, celery and a light touch of garlic), roasted garlic, roasted onion, herb de provence (marjoram, thyme, basil, and rosemary), roasted red pepper, ancho (roasted red and sweet, mild roasted poblano peppers), chipotle (smoked jalapeño pepper), and ranchero (a Southwestern flavor combination of tomato puree base accented with cumin, coriander, black pepper, and other seasonings). They offer gravy and au jus mixtures, as well as a dry roux.

Rounding out their selection are three Oriental cooking sauce concentrates—Szechwan, Sweet 'n' Sour, and Garlic with Black Bean Sauce, all of which are delicious if simply brushed onto chicken as a grilling basting sauce.

In addition to the bases, ALLSERV, Inc., is also a distributor for Maggi seasoning (think light soy sauce flavor with a touch of liquid smoke), Cincinnati chili (canned and seasoning mixes are available for the blend meant, in our opinion, to be served in the five-way style: over spaghetti with a layer of beans, chopped onion, and grated cheddar cheese, although we've improvised and substituted crust for the pasta and made a grilled Cincinnati chili pizza), and Mom's Barbecue Sauce, whose slogan "Only Eve did more for a rib" is indeed true in our opinion.

Mom's is made in 40-gallon batches by a retired auto worker in his Stow, Ohio, home. According to David Sievers of ALLSERV, Inc., "In just a few years, Mom's has been accepted by chefs in top hotels and prestigious country clubs in northeast Ohio," and "has won multiple awards at rib burn-offs and area sauce competitions."

It is a special blend of 18 all-natural ingredients and seasonings with no added preservatives or MSG. Mom's isn't a heavy, tomato-laden, paste-style sauce, but rather is a fat- and cholesterol-free, glaze-like sauce that comes in 18-ounce jars and is available in three flavors, original, spicy and mesquite. In addition to using it to baste your ribs and chicken, you can substitute Mom's in recipes that call for catsup (we've done so when making the stuffed mushrooms and meatballs recipes we mention in Chapter 14), use it as a veggie dip, or add a distinctive flavor to your cheese dips.

Slow-Simmered Flavor

Redi-Base
P.O. Box 846
Whitehall, PA 18052-0846
Customer Service: (800) 820-5121 (Mon.-Fri. 9 a.m. to 8 p.m. EST)
Fax: (610) 820-3947
E-mail: info@redibase.com
Web site: http://www.redibase.com/

Redi-Base bases get their flavor from slow-simmered meat cuts and vegetables (not the end pieces, parts, and bones most often used in bouillon cube preparation). Redi-Base products are lower in sodium content, without sacrificing flavor. This company's vegetable base never needs refrigeration, and you can expand the "shelf life" of the broth bases to a minimum of three years if you store them in the refrigerator.

Their preservative- and MSG-free, paste-style bases include chicken, beef, vegetable, seafood, turkey, and ham, and most also come in reduced sodium content varieties.

For those times you simply don't have the time to make your own rubs and seasonings, Redi-Base also offers a hickory smoke flavor concentrate, a lemon pepper rub and marinade, mesquite smoke flavor concentrate, oreganato rub and marinade, and a Thai rub and marinade.

Smoke Flavor

The Food Smoker Bag

iSi North America, Inc.

Creative Solutions

Phone: (800) 666-6421

Another easy way to add smoke flavor to food is to place it in The Food Smoker Bag from iSi North America, Inc. The Food Smoker Bag is an aluminum envelope padded with a layer of wood chips and sugar. It comes as a set of four bags (one each of hickory, mesquite, alder, and apple) for $15.95 plus shipping from Creative Solutions.

HERB, SPICE, AND PRODUCT RESOURCES

Those who live in larger metropolitan areas can usually find specialty products at gourmet food stores, restaurant supply outlets, or massive food-shopping complexes, such as this Cincinnati area store:

Jungle Jim's

5440 Dixie Highway

Fairfield, OH 45014

Open Mon.-Fri. 8 a.m. to 10 p.m.

Phone: (513) 829-1919

E-mail: jungle@one.net

Web site: http://junglejims.com/

Talk about a huge store! Jungle Jim's now covers more than four acres. Pull into the parking lot and you'll see a gushing waterfall and water-spraying elephants, and hear jungle sounds (not something one generally hears in *any* part of Ohio). While you munch on the vast array of free food samples throughout the store, check out the center store attraction—the Big G Cereal Bowl Band high atop the S.S. Minnow, featuring Trix the Rabbit on keyboard, Honey Bee on percussion, and Lucky the Leprechaun as lead singer and guitarist. (They claim they'll be sure "to get you dancing in the aisles while you shop.") The store offers 800 kinds of beer, more than 6,000 wines, a massive assortment of cheese varieties, and a vast selection of international food, from Afghani to Indonesian. And you don't just find the foodstuffs sitting blandly on a shelf; there's an entire European Gourmet Village, Mexican and Asian markets, and more. It's proof that shopping *The Lazy Way* can be as fun as grilling our way.

The Perfect Lobster

If you don't have a fresh seafood market near you and you're not in the mood to travel to the coast of New England, wade into the Atlantic, and get bashed against the rocks by the waves as you search for that perfect lobster, consider ordering some from The Maine Lobster Company. You can visit their Web site at http://www.mainelobsterco.com, or phone their 24-hour hot line at (207) 828-6226.

Herbs

San Francisco Herb Co.

250 14th St.

San Francisco, CA 94103

Store hours: Mon.-Sat. 10 a.m. to 4 p.m.

Phone: (800) 227-4530 or (415) 861-7174

FAX: (415) 861-4440

Phone times: Mon.-Fri. 9 a.m. to 5 p.m. PST

E-mail: Comments@SFHerb.com

Web site: http://www.sfherb.com/

Neil Hanscomb has owned San Francisco Herb Co. for over 25 years; his wife, Nea, does their Web site and company graphics. Their products are untested by the authors, but considering the time they've been in business, they appear to be an excellent source for dehydrated vegetables, such as green bell pepper and spinach flakes. They also offer a barbecue-and-Cajun spice blend.

Spices

Other mail order and online spice retailers include:

Cibolo Junction Food and Spice Company
3013 Aztec Road NE
Albuquerque, NM 87107
Phone: (800) 683-9628
E-mail: info@cibolojunction.com
Web site: http://www.cibolojunction.com/

The Spice House
1031 N. Old World Third St.
Milwaukee, WI 53203
Phone: (414) 272-0977
Fax: (414) 272-1271
E-mail: spices@thespicehouse.com
Web site: http://www.thespicehouse.com/

Dean and Deluca
2526 E. 36th St. N. Cir
Wichita, KS 67219
Phone: (800) 221-7714
Fax: (800) 781-4050
Web site: http://dd.stores.yahoo.com/dd/

Here is an online and catalog shopping store that offers gourmet foods, dipping oils and vinegars, and spices. This company offers more gourmet kitchen gadgets than they do grilling supplies, but theirs is still a great catalog to have on hand. (Take a look at the spray bottle made especially for turning your choice of cooking oil into your no-stick spray.) Request a catalog (U.S. only) at their Web site or by calling the toll-free number.

Williams-Sonoma
Phone: (800) 621-4097
Web site: http://www.williams-sonoma.com/

The following online and catalog shopping outlet carries grilling accessories such as woks, grill-safe pans, utensils, grill grates, tongs, baskets, and more.

Barbeque People
1819 South University Drive
Davie, FL 33324
Phone: 1-800-371-4866
Web site: http://www.bbqpeople.com/
Web site: http://www.bbqpeople.com/accessories2.html

This company specializes in smokers, but they also carry general grilling supplies as well as mesquite and hickory wood chips.

The Brinkmann Corporation
4215 McEwen Road
Dallas, TX 75244
Phone: (800) 468-5232
Web site: http://www.thebrinkmanncorp.com/

If You Really Want More, Read These

Bittman, Mark. *Fish: The Complete Guide to Buying and Cooking.* New York: Macmillan General Reference, 1994.

Bittman, Mark. *How to Cook Everything: Simple Recipes for Great Food.* New York: Macmillan General Reference, 1998.

Bloom, Carole. *All About Chocolate: The Ultimate Resource to the World's Favorite Food.* New York: Macmillan General Reference, 1998.

California Culinary Academy. *Wrap & Roll: California Culinary Academy.* New York: Macmillan General Reference, 1998.

Crocker, Betty, and Carolyn B. Mitchell. *Betty Crocker's Complete Chicken Cookbook.* New York: Macmillan General Reference, 1994.

Crocker, Betty, and Betty Crocker Editors. *Betty Crocker's Fabulous Fish and Seafood.* New York: Macmillan General Reference, 1995.

Crocker, Betty. *Betty Crocker's Great Grilling Cookbook.* New York: Macmillan General Reference, 1997.

Crocker, Betty, and Betty Crocker Editors. *Betty Crocker's New Choices for Two.* New York: Macmillan General Reference, 1995.

Crocker, Betty Crocker. *Betty Crocker's New Cookbook: Everything You Need to Know to Cook,* (8th Ed). New York: Macmillan General Reference, 1996.

Crocker, Betty Crocker (Editor). *Betty Crocker's Picture Cookbook: The Original 1950 Classic.* New York: Macmillan General Reference, 1998.

Hollis, Martha, and Martha Robinson. *The International Breakfast Book: Greet the Day With 100 Recipes from Around the World.* New York: Macmillan General Reference, 1997.

Holst, Jenna. *Stews: 200 Earthy, Delicious Recipes.* New York: Macmillan General Reference, 1998.

Inc Staff Weight Watchers. *Weight Watchers Slim Ways: Grilling* (Weight Watchers Library). New York: Macmillan General Reference, 1996.

Mitchell, Paulette Mitchell. *The 15-Minute Chicken Cookbook.* New York: Macmillan General Reference, 1997.

Mitchell, Paulette. *The 15-Minute Single Gourmet: 100 Deliciously Simple Recipes for One.* New York: Macmillan General Reference, 1996.

Riely, Elizabeth. *Feast of Fruits: More Than 340 Mouthwatering Recipes for Everything from Apple Chutney To....* New York: Macmillan General Reference, 1996.

Vongerichten, Jean-Georges (Introduction). *Simple Cuisine: The Easy, New Approach to Four-Star Cooking.* New York: Macmillan General Reference, 1998.

Ward, Susie, Claire Clifton, and Jenny Stacey (Contributor). *The Gourmet Atlas.* New York: Macmillan General Reference, 1997.

Weight Watchers Quick Meals. New York: Macmillan General Reference, 1995.

Williams, Sallie Y. *The Complete Book of Sauces.* New York: Macmillan General Reference, 1995.

Wright, Clifford A. *Grill Italian.* New York: Macmillan General Reference, 1996.

If You Don't Know What It Means, Look Here

Basting Brush   A brush used to spread a sauce or marinade over meats as they cook.

Briquettes   The individual pieces of charcoal. They can also have special woods pressed into them for flavor.

Charcoal   The main fuel used in charcoal grills. Comprised of small pieces called briquettes.

Cross-Contamination   When the juices of uncooked meats get on cooking utensils or surfaces. These juices can contain harmful bacteria such as salmonella, or e-coli.

Diffusing Material   On gas grills, a substance such as lava rocks that allows the heat to spread evenly under the cooking area.

Grill   A device used for the cooking of foods. There are different types, like charcoal, gas, and electric.

Grill Basket   A handy item which allows one to place several pieces of meat or vegetables into it for ease in turning during the cooking process.

Grill Cover   Usually made of vinyl, this protects a grill from the elements to keep corrosion from setting in on the exterior of a grill.

Grill Light An attachment for a grill that aids a chef in night cooking.

Grill-Safe Pan Any pan without wooden or plastic handles that can withstand the high temperatures of the grill. The best is a good old cast-iron type.

Grill Thermometer A device that relays the grill's internal temperature, which helps calculate precise cooking times.

Grill Toppers An add-on for a grill used for cooking small or specialty foods.

Grill Umbrella Keeps the food from getting drenched if a rain begins while grilling.

Grilling Mitts Help to prevent burns on the hands, fingers, and lower arms during grilling.

Igniter Switch A push button that causes the fuel to light on a gas grill.

Indirect Cooking Cooking food on a grill without a flame or heat directly underneath the food.

Jerk A special rub or seasoning that originated in Jamaica and the surrounding Caribbean.

Lava Rocks A type of diffusing material. See also Diffusing Material.

Marinade A liquid seasoning for meats, usually containing a tenderizer such as vinegar or citric acid.

Meat Thermometer A tool used to determine the precise inside temperature of meats. The safest way to cook meats to avoid possible sickness due to bacteria.

Pits A grill made out of a combination of brick, blocks, and mortar.

Roasting Rack A special grill attachment for securing large meats or vegetables for indirect cooking.

Rotisserie A device used for cooking a large piece of meat that aids in the turning process.

Skewers   Metal or bamboo "sticks" that allow the cooking of smaller pieces of meats and vegetables.

Smoker Box   A cast-iron box filled with wood chips to add flavor to meats as they cook.

Spatula   A flat ended utensil with a long handle that turns flat pieces of meats and vegetables.

Tongs   A turning utensil for oddly shaped meats and vegetables.

Wood Chips   Used in smoker boxes or directly on charcoal briquettes to add smoke flavor to meats as they cook.

D

It's Time for Your Reward

Once You've Done This:

Answered the "Do You Need This Book?" questions

Taken your kitchen inventory

Gotten all grilling equipment in order and within easy reach

Learned how to make a foil packet

Learned how to build and maintain a proper fire

Simplified the steps necessary to clean up after a grilled feast

Mixed up some rubs to keep on hand

Tasted tahini

Mastered new ways to grill beef

Reward Yourself:

Laugh out loud

Go sing in the sunshine

Tell your worst joke to friends and family

Lounge in the hammock

Sit back and enjoy a cool drink

Look for a four-leaf clover

Recite your favorite childhood poem

Go nuts for a while!

Listen to the ooohs and ahhhs

Tried peaches with your grilled pork instead of applesauce

Whistle "Dixie"

Made a grilled shrimp po-boy

Sandwich in some time to consider yourself a hero for the day

Tried grilling something different

Be bold in all things! Don't wear socks with your sandals

Fixed bratwurst on the grill

Yodel at high volume so you can watch the neighbors' reactions

Made a pizza on the grill

Chase your shadow

Grilled some veggies

Take bagpipe lessons

Licked your fingers without feeling guilty

Snap your fingers and tell your guests that you now have "better traction"

Grilled a midnight snack

Count the stars

Made an entire meal on the grill

Walk around the block

Discovered breakfast outside in the fresh air is as nice as breakfast in bed...sometimes

Stretch out on the lawn and take a nap

Appreciated that grilling can be lots of fun

Smile more

Index

Now you can do these tasks, too!

The Lazy Way

Starting to think there are a few more of life's little tasks that you've been putting off? Don't worry—we've got you covered. Take a look at all of *The Lazy Way* books available. Just imagine—you can do almost anything *The Lazy Way!*

Handle Your Money The Lazy Way
By Sarah Young Fisher and Carol Turkington
0-02-862632-X

Build Your Financial Future The Lazy Way
By Terry Meany
0-02-862648-6

Cut Your Spending The Lazy Way
By Leslie Haggin
0-02-863002-5

Have Fun with Your Kids The Lazy Way
By Marilee Lebon
0-02-863166-8

Keep Your Kids Busy The Lazy Way
By Barbara Nielsen and Patrick Wallace
0-02-863013-0

Feed Your Kids Right The Lazy Way
By Virginia Van Vynckt
0-02-863001-7

*All Lazy Way books are just $12.95!

additional titles on the back!

Learn French The Lazy Way
By Christophe Desmaison
0-02-863011-4

Learn German The Lazy Way
By Amy Kardel
0-02-863165-X

Learn Italian The Lazy Way
By Gabrielle Euvino
0-02-863014-9

Learn Spanish The Lazy Way
By Steven Hawson
0-02-862650-8

Shed Some Pounds The Lazy Way
By Annette Cain and Becky Cortopassi-Carlson
0-02-862999-X

Shop Online The Lazy Way
By Richard Seltzer
0-02-863173-0

Clean Your House The Lazy Way
By Barbara H. Durham
0-02-862649-4

Care for Your Home The Lazy Way
By Terry Meany
0-02-862646-X

Redecorate Your Home The Lazy Way
By Rebecca Jerdee
0-02-863163-3

Stop Aging The Lazy Way
By Judy Myers, Ph.D.
0-02-862793-8

Learn to Sew The Lazy Way
By Lydia Wills
0-02-863167-6

Train Your Dog The Lazy Way
By Andrea Arden
0-87605180-8

Organize Your Stuff The Lazy Way
By Toni Ahlgren
0-02-863000-9

Manage Your Time The Lazy Way
By Toni Ahlgren
0-02-863169-2

Take Care of Your Car The Lazy Way
By Michael Kennedy and Carol Turkington
0-02-862647-8

Get a Better Job The Lazy Way
By Susan Ireland
0-02-863399-7

Cook Your Meals The Lazy Way
By Sharon Bowers
0-02-862644-3

Cooking Vegetarian The Lazy Way
By Barbara Grunes
0-02-863158-7

Get in Shape The Lazy Way
By Annette Cain
0-02-863010-6